THE UNHINGED ALLIANCE

America and the European Community

THE UNHINGED ALLIANCE

ALLIANCE

America
and the European Community

---

by J. ROBERT SCHAETZEL

A Council on Foreign Relations Book
Published by
Harper & Row, Publishers
New York, Evanston, San Francisco
London

THE UNHINGED ALLIANCE: AMERICA AND THE EUROPEAN COMMUNITY. Copyright © 1975 by Council on Foreign Relations, Inc. All rights reserved. Printed in the United States of America. No part of this book may be used or reproduced in any manner whatsoever without written permission except in the case of brief quotations embodied in critical articles and reviews. For information address Harper & Row, Publishers, Inc., 10 East 53rd Street, New York, N. Y. 10022. Published simultaneously in Canada by Fitzhenry & Whiteside, Ltd., Toronto.

FIRST EDITION

Library of Congress Cataloging in Publication Data

Schaetzel, J   Robert, date
  The unhinged alliance.
  (Policy books)
  Includes index.
  1. Europe—Relations (general) with the United
States. 2. United States—Relations (general) with
Europe. I. Council on Foreign Relations. II. Title.
D1065.U5S27   327.73'04   75-4113
ISBN 0-06-013838-6   2-9-76

75 76 77 78 79 10 9 8 7 6 5 4 3 2 1

Policy Books of the Council on Foreign Relations

The purpose of the Policy Books series, of which this is the sixteenth volume, has been to present to the public and to responsible officials in reliatively brief compass the thinking of particularly qualified authors on international issues of major importance to the United States. J. Robert Schaetzel, who served with distinction as the American Ambassador to the European Communities, is such an author, and the topic of relations with Western Europe hardly needs emphasis as a matter of first concern for American foreign policy, and hence as the subject of a "policy book."

The value of a book such as this depends uniquely on the experience and qualities of its author. Ambassador Schaetzel has had a rich first-hand experience, through many administrations, both in the cross-currents of the Washington bureaucracy and in the practice of international negotiation. He appears in these pages not as an ex-diplomat writing his memoirs, but as an analyst drawing on his knowledge of the issues of American-European relations, of the process of policy-making, and of the people involved in that process on both sides. His main concern is with what has gone wrong between the United States and the European Community, the Six now become Nine. His short answer would be "almost everything," but one must read his inside story to find out how and why. That he retains much of his original faith and optimism is an added reason for looking seriously at his recommendations.

During the course of his writing Mr. Schaetzel kept his knowledge up to date through conversations with many persons in Europe and in Washington who are still actively involved. He also had the benefit of the advice of a small group which met for a day at the Council to review and discuss his manuscript. The Council is grateful to the following individuals who took part in that meeting: John C. Campbell, Miriam Camps, James Chace, William Diebold, Robert F. Ellsworth, Robert Kleiman, Edward L. Morse, Andrew J. Pierre, Earl C. Ravenal, Nathaniel Samuels, Eric Stein, Fritz Stern, Richard H. Ullman, Robert W. Valkenier, Robert B. von Mehren, Joseph Zaring.

This is no group product, however, but Robert Schaetzel's own book. He has strong opinions and makes sharp judgments, particularly on the content and the methods of American foreign policy in the past five years. The Council is glad that he has spoken his mind clearly and vigorously. The Council itself takes no responsibility for the book's statements of fact or of opinion. It does take responsibility for the decision to publish it as a contribution to thinking on a subject of central importance both to Americans and to Europeans.

John C. Campbell
Editor

Contents

Chapter I

Introduction

I do not want to add to the impressive accumulation of literature describing the origins or development of the institutions of the emerging European Community, nor to offer one more memoir. My target is narrow: in light of an assessment of the prospects for European unity, and American interests in this phenomenon, to suggest what American policy should be toward a changing Western Europe. Although these suggestions may bear the mark of battle fatigue, they also reflect a native if somewhat battered optimism. When things go wrong or more generally don't go at all, a degree of optimism can be recovered by recalling that the process of unity has undergone its own civil war—and survived.

In this age of pervasive skepticism, especially of things known and inherited, a projection of policies devised in the aftermath of World War II stirs up the charge that another effort is under way to relive the past, to flounder toward the future in a wash of nostalgia. The Atlantic relationship of cooperation instead of conflict, the common security interests, and an expanding web of common responsibilities are properly subject to new cross-examination. I recognize that one must meet the emotional reaction that the postwar policies, by some law of natural obsolescence, must be irrelevant to today's and tomorrow's world. Some elements of the last quarter-century quite obviously cannot be recovered. One was the simplicity of wartime and postwar goals; another, the capacity to strike out in dramatically new directions. While there is need for innovation, this cannot be used as an excuse to ignore those concepts which retain their validity. The ability to identify what was valuable in the past and might be applied to the future is not nostalgia, but an aspect of civilized intelligence.

Some of the same elements of vision and audacity which marked Robert Schuman's proposal of May 1950 for a European Coal and Steel Community were present in former Chancellor Brandt's November 1973 speech to the European Parliament in Strasbourg calling for European union by 1980 and, explicitly, a "European government." In today's atmosphere of negativism an effort is required to recall the powerful case for a united Europe and to appreciate how much has been achieved in less than a generation. The Community has been a major contributor to the fundamental and permanent reconciliation between France and Germany, and has provided the political framework within which a powerful yet democratic Germany could develop as the partner and ally, not the enemy, of its neighbors. The Europeans have devised and now administer a group of novel institutions. The force of the European idea has gathered momentum to the point that, for instance, ex-Foreign Minister Maurice Schumann was moved to advocate the direct election of the European Parliament—while in office he had opposed the Parliament and scorned any notion of election of its members. The force is such that the Italian Communist party endorses the European Community.

Without unity, the strength and growth of the European economy would be problematical. Without unity, there would be slight prospect of a fully responsible role for Europe in world affairs. As Germany has been inextricably involved in the Community's political institutions, so the Community may be equally important in developing the procedures and interlocking interests which can contain and direct the political, social, and economic forces of such transitional societies as Italy.

New arguments for unity, only vaguely foreseen in the 1950s and 1960s, are now advanced. Environmentalists, economists, businessmen, political theorists, and politicians all stress a contracting and increasingly interdependent world. Since centrifugal forces everywhere oppose centripetal necessity, the European experiment may have a critical importance as one of the few contemporary cases of a political process consistent with the reality of interdependence and a counterforce against the destructive reflexes of anachronistic nationalism.

Those who wish America to play a continuing, positive role in international affairs must watch the European Community hopefully, even prayerfully. In this period of America's disenchantment and turning inward, only a strong European partner willing to share burdens and responsibilities can arrest the domestic forces urging withdrawal from world responsibilities.

European unity still conveys the excitement of a political idea far more innovative than the stale doctrines of Marx and Lenin. In less doctrinaire, less self-conscious, or less organized and articulated forms, the Europeans have been contributing to political theory, probing ways in which mature nation states can slowly submerge elements of sovereignty in order to cope with new problems without losing the cultural values or identity of old civilizations. They wish to avoid creating merely a supranational political conglomerate which would further limit contact between those who govern and those they presume to serve. These are large goals; attainment is uncertain. Yet only in the Community is such innovative political experimentation under way.

America's impatience with the past, its current mood of disengagement, and the novelty and drama of new relationships with Russia and China may seem to offer a policy choice. But as the architect of détente, Henry Kissinger, has warned, it would be foolhardy to turn away from the Atlantic relationship. Should the United States or Europe seek to disassociate, one from the other, or from their common stake in the world's trade and payments system, the results would be disastrous for each. There is no evidence that the Soviet Union, in its dark obsession with China or its gestures of good will toward the West, has given up its primordial strategic interest in Central and Western Europe. Any viable international order continues to depend in the first instance on American-European cooperation; it will not be achieved in an atmosphere of Atlantic hostility and cross-purpose. And finally, there is our common cultural heritage, a devotion to the continuing democratic experiment which increasingly seems the odd predilection of a mere handful of the world's population.

The present phase of European integration occurs at a moment of awesome change, with the obsolescence of the postwar system evident but with the new organization and method unclear. Détente with the Soviet Union inevitably weakens the cement of common fear. Other binders—whether they be religion or democracy or the family—lose strength everywhere. As Europe and America drifted apart, Vietnam accelerated a reassessment, in perception and reality, of America's international mission and station. Its economic and military pre-eminence have been lost. The financial crisis of August 1971 threw into stark relief the breakdown of the economic system and the urgent requirement for basic reconstruction if the world were not to slide back into the jungle of trade and financial anarchy. The side-effects of détente, the high costs of defense competing for limited resources, and growing impatience with presumed inequities in the defense burden raise the prospect of a collapse of the Western security system.

The enlarged Community of nine has been condemned, and condemns itself, for failing to seize the opportunities of 1973, for failing to meet the challenges of 1974. This charge seems simplistic; it ignores the magnitude of the problems and fails to appreciate that the drift, inaction, and confusion may, in the perspective of history, be seen rather as a period of necessary consolidation, a time when the European nations further developed a state of mind, a way of thinking about problems in European terms. Impatience and criticism have centered on their evident failures and have discounted the importance of the attitudinal change. While the political process and the politicians have been conditioned, while the European institutions have been tested and found wanting, the public discovered that it was well ahead of its leaders—thus the stage was set for a major move forward.

A basic premise of this book is that the United States must make an urgent effort to establish a foreign policy strategy toward Western Europe, revitalizing America's commitment. We—and Europe as well—still hang half-way between an uneasy hope that somehow or other the old postwar policy framework will still support us and the growing awareness that it does not and cannot. The global metamorphosis is dramatic and comprehensive: a divided, economically frustrated Communist camp, overshadowed by a superpower of overwhelming military strength; a restless, politically unstable, economically threatened, and resentful Third World; a Western Europe painfully organizing itself economically but without a single political voice or even the rudiments of defense unification; a Japan which burst into advanced, industrial society but has yet to find its political and security role. It is unclear whether the crude military balance of the superpowers is transitional or permanent. Economic phenomena and problems push to the forefront of international life. America, no longer confident of its values, distrustful of both private and public institutions, has become atypically pessimistic, suspicious of its friends, tempted again to escape the burdens of international responsibility.

Within this setting an appraisal of American policy toward the enlarged European Community must take place, including assumptions of what this new Europe may look like over the next decade. Why do the Europeans continue to give such singular emphasis to the concept of a united Europe? Why is European unity more than the sum of its visible parts? Why, at the same time, have many Europeans, especially the youth, lost interest in the Community? Has the movement only temporarily stalled, or has the process of unification encountered insuperable obstacles?

It is obviously crucial to re-examine the significance of this European phenomenon to the most basic American political, security, and economic interests, and what we can and should do about it. A central issue is whether Europe, forced by internal or external pressure, will be inclined to organize itself *against* the United States; or indeed, whether the very process of unification makes this inevitable.

The years 1975 and 1976 are critical to Europe: a period of major transition, of mutation, when the institutions, policies, and broad future orientation of the new Community will be determined. This formative, not necessarily thoughtful, process comes at a moment when the United States' capacity for patience or understanding is exceedingly low. Both the internal development of the Community and the nature of its future relations with America are uncertain. The answers to these basic questions will be influenced by the perspective Americans and Europeans achieve—whether it is the long or the short view that dominates. Is there to be a conscious American strategy, or will reaction and improvisation remain in charge? During this critical transition period, patterns will be set by Europe and America which will in all probability endure.

Chapter II

Contrasts: 1950 and 1975

There is more than a generation gap between the Western Europe of today and that of 1950. The issues confronting the Europeans in 1950—Stalin and the Cold War, shattered economies, a dollar gap, Berlin, whither Germany—had a simple clarity. Even if our assessments and solutions were wrong, as the revisionists would have us believe, at least problems with sharp outlines facilitated decision and action. The war's destruction brought in its wake both a loss of faith in the inherited political structures and a willingness of victor and vanquished to strike out in new directions. Europeans, such as Jean Monnet, have envied America's capacity to change, especially in contrast with the embedded, almost immovable European societies. The war, for a moment, loosened these tightly drawn bonds.

The awesome yet simple goal of reconstruction and recovery brought human energies and governmental institutions into rare harmony. Excessive importance has been given to the incentive of the external threat, but certainly Stalin's brutal actions within the Soviet Union and Eastern Europe sharpened European fears and stimulated action.

The United States emerged from the war confident, bursting with economic power, possessing overwhelming military strength, released from its isolationist heritage, and willing to experiment and lead. Out of this creative ferment came the United Nations system, the Marshall Plan, foreign aid, the trade and payments system, and a country ready to support efforts to create a prosperous and peaceful international order. Such a world seemed within reach.

Critics have ignored the fact that America did not employ its incomparable power to divide Europe for the purpose of dominance and exploitation. During the crucial Truman years, with the creation of the International Monetary Fund, the World Bank, and the General Agreement on Trade and Tariffs (GATT), there emerged a self-conscious effort to put together an economic world of rules and institutions. The Marshall Plan, with its objective an independent and self-reliant Europe, was consistent with this policy. It might have been otherwise.

The Western Europe of 1975 could not have been foreseen in 1945 or even 1955. In contrast with the desperation and doubt of the postwar period, the continent today bears the mixed blessings and curses of economic affluence: high incomes, consumer economies, environmental pollution, inflation, depopulated farm lands, and suffocating cities. But the willingness to experiment and to accept change has waned in the tide of material consumption.

The warm breezes of Brehznev replaced the cold winds of Stalin. Fruitless, acrimonious East-West meetings were superseded by the Berlin agreement and congenial gatherings in Helsinki of Eastern and Western foreign ministers. Within the framework of Communist orthodoxy, the Eastern Europeans sought for the means to develop further their economic relations with the West.

Radical but still obscure changes have occurred in the relationship between Europe and America, and in their basic attitudes. The intimacy of the war and postwar period, the unquestioning assumption of broad common interests, the leader-follower relationship have all become historical oddities, remarked upon by children on both sides of the Atlantic to whom the war against the Axis powers and defense and security are little more than the fretful worries of old men.

Until 1973 Western Europe remained divided. In January 1963 the French veto of the first British application for membership in the Community had set off another of Europe's debilitating, fratricidal battles. A long decade later, with the British uneasily inside, essentially all of democratic Western Europe was finally free to apply its energies to constructive development, if it chose to do so.

Despite sharp alterations in the political and psychological landscape, however, there lie durable features which have not significantly shifted since the 1950s. Europeans still crave influence and status commensurate with their interests and history. De Gaulle epitomized this desire but tragically lacked the vision to see that it could never again be achieved on the basis of the eighteenth- and nineteenth-century pattern of small nation-states. Britain's tragedy was less dramatic but no less traumatic. Until 1961 it clung to the belief that an England without power or empire could maintain a world position on the foundation of illusion, Commonwealth, and a "special relationship" with the United States.

The question remains whether the on-coming generations will share this yearning for European influence. While indifferent to power or status, the concern of the young in relieving world poverty and in improving the quality of life may bring them to realize that these goals cannot be attained in the absence of a more effective organization of Europe's human, economic, and political resources. Assertion by their elders that European unity supplies the answer is not enough. Youth's impatience with, if not distaste for, all government carries over to slackening enthusiasm for the existing European Community. The Community appears as merely a further example of the ease with which ideas and institutions can be drained of excitement and promise.

A second feature common to 1950 and 1975 is the determination to preserve the diversity of European traditions, cultures, languages, and communities. As unification moves beyond pure rhetoric the dilemma sharpens: Is an effective Community compatible with the constructive diversity the European nations wish to preserve?

Third, Europeans in 1950 were not interested in reproduction of the American political system, nor are they today. Some will employ the word "federal," but loosely, without implying a political structure modeled on the American experience. Ironically, Europe has borrowed from America the extra-constitutional increment to executive power as seen in the development of the Executive Office of the President. Pompidou, Heath, and Brandt, in their own ways and within the parliamentary system, initiated moves in a similar direction. Accretions to executive power are not necessarily a contribution to a European federal system. Indeed, it could further strengthen the national states at the head-of-government level, indirectly hindering the development of stronger Community institutions.

Another durable feature is the almost universal European desire to preserve the existing Western defense system. For the foreseeable future, NATO, American involvement on the ground, and American commitment of strategic forces are irreplaceable. The problem is less a matter of differing perceptions of basic Western security requirements, or of differing defense policies, than of political will. Do the European political leaders have the authority and capacity to persuade colleagues and parliaments to allocate the necessary resources?

The U.S.S.R., China, and European Unity

The Soviet Union's strategic approach to European unity has been a rock of consistency. Since the days of Czarist agents in seventeenth-century Poland, European animus and division have spelled security for Russia; a West coalescing or united has meant danger, as Professor Jerzy Lukaszewski has documented. He quotes F. I. Tyutchev's assertion of 1864: "The only natural policy for Russia vis-à-vis the West must be, not an alliance with one or another of these powers, but their disunion and division; for it is only when they are divided that they are not hostile—never, of course, by conviction, but out of powerlessness."[1] Lenin picked up this thread of ancient Russian policy in his famous article of September 1915, "On the Slogan of the United States of Europe."

Soviet tactical flexibility led, momentarily, to reluctant acceptance of what Khrushchev thought could no longer be ignored. In 1962 he published an article which said that "The imperialists, in spite of their contradictions, succeeded in achieving on the international scale, although incompletely, their economic cooperation in certain important sectors.... It would be giving proof of levity and political myopia not to pay attention to the designs and machinations of the file-leaders of European integration."[2] A decade later, in a statement to a trade union congress, Brezhnev took another small step and seemed to bring the Soviet Union to the verge of formal recognition. But Moscow was not yet ready. Only in 1974 and 1975 did Soviet and Commission officials get down to semi-formal, if still inconclusive, discussion of some relationship between the Community and the U.S.S.R.

The reasons for Soviet opposition to European unity have been elaborated in both foreign propaganda and tracts for internal U.S.S.R. consumption. In addition to the historical interest in Western disunity the Russians fear economic disadvantage. The coincidence of a declining Western European market for the traditional Eastern exports of agricultural products and raw materials with a Community farm policy that

1. *Le Monde*, Oct. 2–3, 1970.
2. Ibid.

smacks of autarky has confirmed this fear. Moscow has also been unnerved by the threat to Communist solidarity posed by the equivocation of several of the national Communist parties in the Community member states, especially the bourgeois pragmatism of the Italians. Members of the Italian Communist party not only sit in the European Parliament in Strasbourg but come well prepared and participate actively in its work. The Russians can envision the corruption of sister Communist parties in the East. The mere existence of the Community is painful. How is it that capitalist societies, instead of being at one another's throats, are submerging national sovereignty in common interests, a political phenomenon which challenges fundamental Communist dogma?

A clue to current Soviet tactics can be gleaned from an article in *Pravda*. "Europe needs real security on an all-European basis. It is essential that she develop equal cooperation of all countries. All-European economic cooperation naturally in no way excludes regional cooperation. The 'Common Market' in Western Europe and the Council for Mutual Economic Assistance in Eastern Europe are the realities of our times. However, the far-reaching development of the 'Common Market,' the efforts to prevent its members from developing normal trade relations with the socialist countries, particularly the efforts of certain circles to give this Organization the character of a political, or even military grouping, have nothing to do with the officially stated aims of regional economic cooperation. It is on that side of the question that the attention of public groups working for all-European cooperation is now turning."[3]

The devices the Soviet Union employs to deal with an enlarged and economically powerful Community are apparent. The Soviet goal is to restrict the Community to the status of a "trading bloc." To this end, pressure can be applied at several points. Initially, the Conference on Security and Cooperation in Europe seemed a useful instrument. By blurring issues with obscure language and resolutions, the Conference, made up of nation-states, perhaps could be used to play upon the desire of the Western states to maintain their bilateral relations with the U.S.S.R. and especially with the Eastern European countries. Détente is also a handy device. A submerging of the military threat weakens the impulse of the Western Europeans to unify. Conversely, any Western movement toward political or defense unification can be attacked and decried as harmful to an all-European accommodation.

3. *Pravda*, Aug. 25, 1972.

The Russians can use the leverage of Western Europe's interest in finding means of easing the lot of the Eastern Europeans, of offering relationships to supplement but not to supplant those the East must have with the U.S.S.R. With this humane objective in mind, the Community members seek to encourage contacts between East and West, especially in the economic area. Moscow has contrived an elegant torture for the West Europeans. It says, "If you insist on presenting yourselves as a bloc or a community, as you have, for instance, in the Conference on European Security and Cooperation, then the East will reply in kind through Comecon."

None knows better than the Eastern Europeans the absence of similarity between the European Community and Comecon. A few European observers thought that the tentative rapprochement between Prague, Bucharest, and Belgrade in the summer of 1968 might contain the seeds of some analagous organization in the East, but the Soviet invasion of Czechoslavakia in August effectively killed that tender flower. True symmetry would have the Soviets, in their relations with their immediate Communist neighbors, follow American behavior toward Western European unity in standing aside, even encouraging Eastern European union and independence.

The primary Russian objective in coping with the European Community is to prevent any further political development—certainly any movement in the field of defense. Such moves would be fought as a threat to détente. Western governments are vulnerable to this charge since it arms the domestic opposition looking for ammunition with which to attack those in power. The Russians have a special hold on the West German government in the threat to negate the agreements on which Bonn had expended so much effort and political capital and run such internal risks.

It would be equally surprising if Moscow in its attempts to curb Western European unification did not exploit its new relationships with Washington. There have been delicate suggestions by the Soviets that America and Russia have suffered common injury from the Community's restrictive agricultural policy, that the superpowers have similar interests in opposing the European Community's special deals with the nations of the Mediterranean and Africa, and, even more piously, that Russia and America have common interest in a multilateral world as opposed to one of blocs. Can there be a Soviet official so unimaginative as to overlook the mischief to be done in encouraging among already uneasy Western Europeans the suspicions of converging Soviet and American interests?

The Russians believe it is in their national interest to ignore the Community as long as possible; when forced to accept the inevitable, they will circumscribe the recognition. This approach has several advantages; it is consistent with established Soviet gospel; it keeps alive the hope that perhaps the Community will fall apart; it allows time for the solvent of détente and some "all-European alternative" to do their work; it makes the Western European task of unification more difficult; not least, nonrecognition keeps the Eastern European satellites in line.

One aspect of the 1950 picture which had wholly changed by 1974 was the role of China. In the fractured Communist world Moscow cannot ignore the European policy of its eastern neighbor. The Chinese government in recent years has frequently reiterated its support of Western European unification. Chou En-lai, for instance, in June 1971 clearly and precisely offered warm encouragement to the European Community, primarily as a means for Western Europe to free itself from the hegemony of the two superpowers. The Chinese Vice-Minister of the Foreign Ministry, when in London in November 1972, responded unambiguously to a request for Chinese reaction to British membership in the Community: China supported without reservation, indeed with enthusiasm, the enlargement as well as the further development of the Community. And one can only wonder at Pompidou's reaction to Chou En-lai's more pointed declarations during the French President's visit to Peking in favor of European economic, political, and military integration.

Chinese encouragement of cooperation and unity among the Eastern European nations is less well known in the West, but is entirely logical. In each case it is the means for small countries to escape oppression of the great powers. There is also a special bond between China and Eastern Europe. The small nations of Eastern Europe were never party to the sordid European, Japanese, and American imperialist adventures in China in the nineteenth century. The Poles, for example, had the same vicarious satisfaction from the 1905 defeat of Czarist forces in Asia that they must have today from the hard ideological and geographic confrontation between China and the Soviet Union. Furthermore, the main thrust of Chinese foreign policy runs directly counter to the Brezhnev policy; it encourages rather than seeks to stifle ideological diversity.

China holds and can play at will the wild card of formal recognition of the European Community. Peking has yet to translate its general support of unification into specific action. China methodically negotiated bilateral agreements with each of the Western European states, culminating in 1972 with the negotiations with the Federal Republic of Germany. In this diplomatic process the Chinese turned back all inquiries about when or even whether they would appoint an ambassador to the European Community. They can move when it suits their convenience, presumably when it would embarrass Moscow and assist the Eastern Europeans. In the meantime the Chinese embassy to Belgium provides a convenient base for a large staff which examines and tries to understand the Community and its mysterious processes.

European Views on Unity

Except in Denmark and Great Britain, every poll that canvasses continental European opinion shows strong, popular support for the idea of European unity. But what does "unity" mean? The sheer generality of the word brings together strange bedfellows. At the level of political abstraction, de Gaulle's call for a Europe for the Europeans approximated Monnet's simple, tirelessly reiterated appeal for an independent, united Europe capable of speaking with one voice. The profound intellectual quarrel of these two Frenchmen turned less on the ultimate end than on deep disagreement over the means.

De Gaulle could only envision a Europe unified by the dominance of one nation-state. To Monnet it was this quest for domination that brought Europe its tragic history of devastating wars and the destruction of its capacity to influence the world about it. De Gaulle saw government in terms of authority, the mystic leader guiding his quarrelsome, if not foolish, people. Monnet, impatient in his own way with some of the practices of democracy, identified institutions as the crucial issue in the political process, with the role of political leadership that of creating and sustaining these political bodies. De Gaulle's genius was to establish a "constitutional monarchy" and to employ modern techniques of public manipulation to reinforce its political structure, all in order to pursue eighteenth-century dreams. For Monnet, European unity in the form of the new Community would eliminate once and for all the original sin of dominance.

Where are the Europeans going and by what route? The three treaties for the European Coal and Steel Community, Euratom, and the European Economic Community, the constitutional base of the present European Community, offer a point of departure. But a logical evolution from this foundation has been stymied by more than a decade of dispute over interpretation of the treaties and their execution. France's obduracy and threats forced its partners to accept the extra-legal suppression of majority voting, a key feature of the European constitution. The 1969 and 1972 summit meetings laid down new Community goals, including monetary union, in brave, albeit general, language. But the hardest questions remain to be answered. The European Parliament lacks authentic legislative powers. Despite the pronouncements of the 1975 Paris summit meeting, the member states have made no serious effort to restore majority voting, the absence of which two centuries ago rendered impotent the American Confederation of States. National bureaucracies resist granting the Commission, the Community's executive body, real if limited authority. There is endless talk of political union, but little substance, and, since the death of the European Defense Treaty in 1954, no consideration of the Community's role in defense.

Over the past twenty years, some of the stimuli which led to the development of the Community have disappeared, reducing the momentum toward unity. Europeans no longer sense a clear and present external threat. If a pressing danger is necessary to move peoples to peaceful revolutionary action, is there a substitute for the menace of Stalin? Jean-Jacques Servan-Schreiber, among others, suggested that the United States' technological dominance could cast America in this role. Some Europeans believe a brisk commercial war across the Atlantic or the precipitous withdrawal of American forces could be the catalyst for greater unity. There are those who feel that the poor European performance in the threshold industries of computer technology, space, and advanced aircraft will force Europe to turn to further unity. For Europeans who give priority to other positive goals—improved environment, the quality of life, assistance to the developing countries—unity and the effective mobilization of latent European resources seem to be the only answer. The humiliation of living in the shadow of the superpowers, of knowing that the world's crucial issues are being discussed and even settled without European participation, is another possible impetus. Finally, as Europe bent before the economic storms of 1974 (inflation, massive payments deficits, faltering growth, and an energy crisis), there were those who saw this as more than a stimulus. It was an imperative demand for unity.

The excitement of the Schuman Plan years has dissipated. Partly responsible have been the inevitable, niggling technical work of economic unification and the faceless bureaucracy which does the Community's bargaining. The Community today does not offer the political base for a charismatic leader who might wish to relate the dreary daily work to political ideals and thereby rekindle popular enthusiasm. Indeed, Community institutions seem designed to prevent the emergence of such a "European" leader. Not only do the member states inhibit the natural development of the Commission, which might be such a political base, but the two-year limit on the term of the President (with perhaps a one-year extension grudgingly offered) stifles even this limited potentiality. A more precise political vision or a specific political program could counterbalance the slogging technical work, the Kafkaesque bureaucracy, and the absence of an acknowledged Community leader.

Although general popular support for European unity has been remarkably durable, the support now comes from different quarters and in differing intensity. The continental socialist parties and labor unions which at the outset opposed the Coal and Steel Community today endorse the European Community, despite labor's restlessness with the Community's procrastination over those social and economic programs considered vital to their constituencies. Early enthusiasm for the Community came from the young; today, European youth is apathetic or even hostile. Businessmen, cool twenty years ago, now want wider and faster integration. National governments which conceived the Community and make the process possible—especially France and Germany —came to view Community institutions with the same reservations Dr. Frankenstein was to have for his handiwork. No political leader or government can lay responsibility for the slow progress of European unity at the door of a hostile public.

The Economic Road to Integration

Monnet postulated that revolutionary change culminating in full European union could be achieved by a series of moves in the various economic sectors. As each economic step was taken, it would create an imbalance that would force movement in related areas, giving irreversible momentum to the whole integration process and leading to eventual political union. During these last years when the pace of unification has slowed, some disciples of a united Europe have come to question the validity of this postulate. The momentum of economic integration has been broken, and today even among the true believers, the theory that political unity will emerge almost automatically from full economic integration seems, at best, arguable. In fact, in 1973 there emerged a consensus that the entire process of integration would be stalemated in the absence of actions by the Community in the political field. Alternative dangers were perceived: the first, that as Europe attained a high level of economic affluence and the public commitment to the *status quo* grew, energies would slacken, complacency dominate, and Europe would lack the will to succeed in the even more difficult fields of politics and defense. The second danger, underscored by the reaction to the 1974 energy and financial crisis, was that Europe would instinctively react nationally and unilaterally, with only lip service to Community obligations or interests. Indeed, as Europe struggled with recession many observers questioned whether any progress was possible in such an adverse economic environment.

It is, however, too early to write off Monnet's theories. In a sense, the abortive scheme for economic and monetary union and, conversely, the belated agreement to proceed with regional policy appear to vindicate him. The Conference on European Security and Cooperation and the Nixon-Kissinger plea for a new "Atlantic Charter" forced the Community to behave as a unit, despite the reluctance of some member states. The persistently vague discussion about political union, the endless speculation of where to begin vesting the Parliament with additional power, may perversely support Monnet's argument by demonstrating that a non-economic approach does not work. In short, the basic impulse still comes out of the economic area, for instance, from the discontent of interest groups with inequities caused by partial integration. Even the unhappiness with institutions and procedures stems from the Community's incapacity to deal efficiently with economic problems.

A Toynbeean view of European unification would divide its history into negative and positive eras. The European Community has now passed through the first, the negative, period of its development, which required the dismantling of tariffs, the merging of national agriculture programs in a Common Agricultural Policy (CAP), the elimination of local inhibitions on the free movement of workers, and the development of rules of establishment. That task was the less difficult one because the barriers were obvious; the treaties generally identified specific targets and laid down schedules to achieve these goals. For the positive stage of Community development, more formidable problems are raised and the existing treaties are either only suggestive or silent. Community policies on technology, energy, and environment, for instance, promise to cut into sensitive areas of national social and economic life. This is one reason for the slow pace at which the Community is now moving.

After years of expert advice and pleading, after endless reports, the member governments duly committed themselves to the goal of economic and financial union by 1980. The Treaty of Rome intentionally slid over financial matters. During the 1957 negotiations, prospects for the Common Market were far from bright. The hopes of the "Europeans" rode on Euratom and the glamorous new field of atomic energy. The officials who elaborated the treaties under the direction of Paul-Henri Spaak believed that if the already dubious prospects for governmental ratification of the Common Market treaty were further burdened by financial provisions the treaty would surely fail. The Spaak team was well aware of the hostility of central bankers and ministers of finance to the concept of a European Economic Community. But, in fact, the Common Market became the engine of the whole integration process. With the customs union and the Common Agricultural Policy established, there was little choice but to round out the Community with common policies in the monetary field. Recurrent European, and then internal, financial crises converted the European financial community from indifference or suspicion to outright support.

The full implications of monetary union did not escape the Europeans. The elimination of currency margins, a central bank, and a European reserve system imply nothing less than full economic union. If there were to be economic union, then there would have to be common social policies, limited variations in rates of inflation and deflation among the member states, coordination, compromise, and even synthesis of national budgetary policies and programs. There could be no financial and economic union without strong institutions. We shall never know whether these ambitious plans of 1972 ever had a chance. This great economic design was postulated on a dynamic European economy, and the anticipated problems were the crucial questions of political will and capacity for concerted action.

Despite its sudden conversion to historic bric-a-brac, economic and monetary union did point up a doctrinal dispute common to most Community debate. Should progress be made through small, concrete, institution-building steps, or by means of increasingly intense consultation and intergovernmental coordination and cooperation? It was natural that Paris, under the spell of Gaullism, would play on the instinctive reservations of other member states in regard to vesting additional authority in Community institutions. Thus French policy and the predilections, and fatigue, of others gave a certain plausibility to the coordination-cooperation approach which it might otherwise not deserve.

The European Community Today

Friend and foe acknowledge the sluggish pace of the Community. Despairing supporters insist that it must begin to move or it will die; others see stagnation as proof that the process of unification has run its course. Even in such fields as company law and industrial policy, basic to the establishment of conditions necessary if the Europeans are to derive the full benefits from the Community, progress has been essentially nil. In a Europe dependent on imported fuel, Euratom, with its research facilities, experts, and technology, has lain perpetually at death's door. Face to face with the energy crisis, first the Council of Ministers and then the heads-of-government at Copenhagen temporized over any Community energy policy at all. It is a story of endless discussion, stalemate, and inaction.

There are both rational and irrational reasons for this impasse. Resistance to the transfer of responsibility, or, if you like, sovereignty, from entrenched bureaucracies and governments is an immutable, gravitational force. Despite the catalogue of unfinished business, the Community has had its successes, for example, in trade and agriculture; it has become a major factor in European economic and political life. This very achievement produces, by the laws of governmental mechanics, a counterreaction. The young, one-time Belgian Minister of Finance, Professor Vlerich, fresh from academic life, said that he now knew where the real enemies of European integration were: "Right in my own ministry." These functionaries devote themselves to frustrating Community decisions, even the will of their own ministers.

Appropriate credit goes to the French for this state of affairs. Behind a façade of rhetorical support, France for over a decade waged a skillful and persistent ideological battle against the Community, with its sharpest attack levelled against the Commission.

The conflict reached its peak when the Commission, under the presidency of Walter Hallstein, boldly decided in 1965 to present the Council of Ministers with a "package" defining the common financing of the agricultural policy, providing for early completion of the customs union, creating the Community's independent resources by transfer of levies on agricultural products and of industrial duties, enhancing the powers of the European Parliament and, not least, those of the Commission as well. The Commission's audacity infuriated de Gaulle and led to the serious "Luxembourg crisis" and a French boycott of the Community institutions for more than six months. In addition to humbling the Commission, de Gaulle was determined to redirect the development of the Community. Its intergovernmental character was to be assured by eliminating majority voting. Almost by rote, the French reaction to any proposition was, first, "Why should the Community do it?"; then, if the proposition had to be explored, "Assign the task to the Committee of Permanent Representatives"; finally, if the pressure for action was irresistible, "Establish the program independent of the existing Community institutions."

The French did not create, they *rallied*, the forces of nationalism. As Paris passed each Community proposal through the fine screen of immediate French national interest, other governments fretted, then imitated. This approach insured that wider Community interest would be lost from view. In an atmosphere of national self-gratification, the practical politicians who ignored local interests risked becoming former politicians. The result was that, in Community business, lines were drawn close to the outer limits of purely national and short-term interests.

During the critical years 1972 and 1973, special circumstances inhibited movement in the political and defense fields. In France, slowly emerging from the cocoon of Gaullism, Pompidou was unprepared to expose himself to attack from the "ultras" by endorsing Community responsibility in any area not included in the existing treaties, especially subjects as contentious as these. In Britain, Heath faced determined Labour Party opposition to the whole idea of European unity as well as sniping from his own right wing led by Enoch Powell. To raise defense and foreign policy as immediate Community business during negotiations for British entry would have offered additional targets to the enemies of Great Britain's participation in European unification. In the light of this situation the "good Europeans" temporized.

But foreign policy could not be totally ignored in view of the decisions reached at the 1969 Hague summit meeting. Under the six-month rotation system it fell to Belgium to chair the Council of Ministers. As a result, that most skillful Belgian diplomat Vicomte Davignon decided that it was the moment to produce a mouse. Out of the discussions he led with the political experts from the member states there emerged a loosely organized committee, working without a secretariat and without institutional pretensions. The immediate problem before the "Davignon Committee" at the time was to avoid complicating further Pompidou's already difficult situation and the problems Heath had on the right and left, and to concentrate on the primary goal of British entry. The Davignon Committee remained a holding action until the 1972 summit meeting and the entry of the new members in 1973 freed the Community from these special restraints.

The loose informality of the Davignon Committee is in sharp contrast with the political notions of the Community's founding fathers. The designers of the Coal and Steel Community and, subsequently, Euratom and the EEC included two ingenious measures to save the Community from the impotence of traditional intergovernmental bodies: first, a Commission with special and exclusive powers of initiative, reinforced by obligating the Council of Ministers to accept or reject its proposals or to return them to the Commission for amendment, and by vesting the power of enforcement in the Commission as well; second, qualified majority voting. Pressure from the member states through the Council of Ministers has compromised the authority of the Commission through the assignment of many of these tasks to the Committee of Permanent Representatives and to *ad hoc* committees under the Council itself. Today unanimity is the rule rather than majority voting.

The institutional riddle—how to get efficiency and decisions while maintaining a proper balance among the various Community organs and between them and the member governments—is at the heart of the crisis facing the integration movement. Much of the loss of support for the Community among Europeans and Americans has a common root: its ineffectiveness as a political body.

Some skeptics obscure this complex issue by insisting that it is nothing more than the tiresome pursuit of that will-o'-the-wisp "supranationality" by committed "Europeans." In fact, the real problem is reached well before one approaches fine points of political theology. The British, newly arrived in 1973, in awe described the Brussels institutions as a gigantic administrative machine with innumerable rapidly moving parts dominated by a massive flywheel spinning at terrifying speed. But it is all illusory. Despite the perpetual motion, the Community machine, like some vast steamroller, progresses in centimeters. The enlarged Community must decide whether the Europeans are to be helpless victims of this complicated machine, or whether they can control and direct their own bureaucratic creation.

Revitalizing Community Institutions

If the Community is to satisfy even the most modest ambitions of its members, it must be able to make plans, decide policy, carry on international discussions, and negotiate. Nine separate governments in loose coalition cannot accomplish these common tasks. Nor can the Council of Ministers, nor the Committee of Permanent Representatives. The process of elimination leaves only the European Commission. In addition to its vital executive functions, the Commission is the indispensable institution to reflect "community" interests and the "community" conscience. To limit further the Commission's already restricted mandate drastically worsens the odds against development of the Community and success of the integration movement.

There are various explanations for the decline of the Commission. Responsibility cannot be laid exclusively at the door of jealous or indifferent national governments. The Hallstein Commission acquired unique prestige, as the drafters of the Treaty of Rome intended. Strongly led, it also included a number of notably competent and powerful commissioners—Marjolin, Rey, and Mansholt—who had the wit to work together and formed the nucleus for an effective Commission. But events—implacable French hostility following the Luxembourg crisis of 1965, new personalities, and very different external conditions—conspired to diminish its authority. Among political scientists the commission system has acquired notoriety for its innate inefficiency; when lifted to the international level, the inherent weaknesses of this political institution are magnified manyfold—perhaps by nine.

If the Commission of the Community of nine is to fulfill the several special and indispensable functions—initiator, spokesman, negotiator—it must recover the ground that has been lost. It must behave again as a collective body, a political entity with something close to the cabinet responsibility of the parliamentary government. When President Mansholt in 1972 urged his colleagues to go forth in the world and speak their independent minds, he may have catered to psychic needs of the commissioners; but the result was public confusion and further erosion of the Commission's status.

The Council of Ministers remains the central element in the Community structure, with a monopoly of authority to decide but without the ability to execute or administer. As the Community has evolved, the Council has become, in effect, the European legislative body, with the ultimate power to appropriate money and to determine Community programs. As the Community extends its reach into new economic areas, separate councils come into play, supplementing those of foreign, agriculture, finance, and transport ministers. There is no overarching institutional device by which the separate fields of activity can be monitored to assure the compatibility of one with the other, or with other Community policies and programs; or to assure that the general Community interest is not lost in the satisfaction of a special interest, such as agriculture. In theory, the Council of Foreign Ministers is the superior body. Actually, these foreign ministers lack the specialized knowledge which would enable them to intervene decisively in the various technical fields. But, more to the point, foreign ministers are generally in a weak tactical position to challenge or override cabinet colleagues on substantive issues —finance, industrial policy, agriculture—for which the latter are responsible. One must not forget that these same colleagues are fellow politicians as well.

A crucial point in reforming the Council is the decision-making process. Various rationalizations are advanced in support of the current practice of unanimity; to override a "vital interest" of a member state could lead to the destruction of the Community; majority voting would encourage unprincipled coalitions among member governments and logrolling on a vast scale, something the current consensus-building and unanimity allegedly avoid; the new members, in making their difficult adjustment to Community life, cannot be denied what the old members have enjoyed. Yet the absence of majority voting makes the work of the Council infinitely more difficult. In addition to the time consumed in the search for unanimity, irresistible pressures bear down on each member state to exercise the veto implicit in this practice in order to satisfy the most extreme national demands. Without majority voting, the lubricant of the democratic process—fight the "good fight" and from time to time be defeated by the majority—is lacking.

One example will illustrate the damaging effects of current practice. The Davignon Committee was developing a Community position on the Conference on European Security and Cooperation. The life of the Danish government, with its unstable coalition of contending political factions, was dependent on the support of a splinter group. This small party, by threats to withdraw from the government and thus bring it down, was able to force its own foreign policy views on the coalition. As a result, the Danish delegation in Brussels advanced, and refused to modify, a position unrepresentative of general Danish opinion. Presumably the Danish delegation would have been grateful if the majority-vote principle had prevailed. Then the Danes could have presented their extreme position; it would have been considered and voted down by the Political Committee; policy generally acceptable to the majority would have been agreed upon; and, not least important, the Danish government could have faced its irate political faction with clean hands.

As the Council emerged at the unchallenged power center of the Community, this institution became in turn the means of frustrating action, of defending national interest, and of systematically degrading the Commission. A political system of awesome inefficiency has resulted, offering incentives for obstruction and inducements to extremism. Unable to ignore longer this state of affairs, the heads-of-government at the 1972 summit turned the matter back for solution to the culprit, the Council. By then, not even the Council could gainsay the political mess. Moreover, the advent of the Giscard government eased French rigidity and set the stage for possible reform, based on recommendations presented earlier by Walter Scheel, as president of the Council, and the Commission's President, François-Xavier Ortoli. At the Council of Ministers meeting in June 1974 a consensus began to form on two crucial points: at least partial abandonment of the custom of unanimity in decision-making and granting more power to the Commission.

Goads to Decision and Action

One may wonder how the Community, impeded by these natural and unnatural barriers, has managed to advance at all. It has refined the process of periodic crises, reaching decisions through exhaustion at the end of marathon ministerial sessions. British negotiators subjected to this procedure in 1971 and 1972 found it both exhilarating and frightening. The process could produce through total fatigue a certain clarity of mind and decision. But it carries too the danger of handing victory not to the reasoned case but to the strongest constitution.

In addition to the obvious risks, there are limitations to this technique. Can crises be controlled, or are they apt to get out of hand? In view of the dimensions of recent internal and likely future external events—a breakdown of the monetary system, a new mercantilism, upheavals in the Mediterranean, another energy crisis, sharp change in Soviet policy, sudden withdrawal of substantial American troops—the Community's system is ill-adapted to cope either rapidly or wisely with problems of such magnitude. The crisis-stimulus is a blunt instrument. Its effectiveness is greatest when the Community faces imminent inescapable issues —such as agricultural price decisions tied to the farm cycle or Community decisions enabling officials to meet the time schedule of international negotiations. In contrast, it is difficult to engineer and then effectively employ a crisis to produce decisions on the major and longer-range problems facing the Community: energy or technological policy, the role of the Community in defense, even urgent issues related to monetary policy. Despite the perils inherent in this technique and the hint that procedural reform may be coming, it seems likely that progress-by-crisis will continue to play a significant role in the life of the Community.

Specific deadlines were a device built into the basic treaties as a conscious means of budging the inanimate. The Commission, the Council of Ministers, and the occasional summit meetings all employ the deadline as a way of overcoming inertia. Unfortunately, as in the case of the common commercial policy toward the Communist countries, the Community has shown that *in extremis* it can find excuses to ignore deadlines, even those prescribed in the treaties.

Summit meetings of heads-of-government have become, almost by accident, a new Community instittuion. One of the major purposes of these meetings has been to deal with the paralysis that curses the Community. Some European theoreticians fear and deplore this innovation as a threat to the integrity of the Community system. There are reasons for the concern. Periodic summit meetings may inhibit the growth and normal evolution of the Commission, the Council of Ministers, and the Parliament. These Community bodies, conscious of a supreme, if *ad hoc,* committee composed of heads-of-government, will tend to defer decisions and hand up to the summit matters which should be handled within the system established by the treaties. This is precisely what happened, for instance, before the December 1973 summit. Decisions made in the course of occasional heads-of-government meetings have a tendency to be capricious or superficial, arrived at without proper preparatory work or systematic deliberation.

Nonetheless most Europeans accept, with varying enthusiasm, the summit device. It is almost the only means at this time of getting action and decision and also of dealing with substantive matters beyond the explicit competence of the existing Community. For example, the treaties are silent with respect to foreign policy and defense; and authority is, at best, implicit regarding environment. To bring such matters within the Community orbit requires new decisions by the member governments. Furthermore, heads-of-government have the full range of political authority and, if they wish to use it, the capacity to conclude with their colleagues complex compromise packages—agreement on agriculture can be traded for a decision on energy; both can be used to bargain for an agreement of regional policy. Finally, in a mood of desperation, many Europeans turn to the summit as a last resort in their search for the means to restore flagging political will and momentum for the Community.

Of the many dangers confronting the integration process, the most acute is the Community's difficulty, almost incapacity, to act, to decide. This disease, endemic in all democratic societies, has the side-effect of sapping public confidence in government. The problem must be met by the Community if it is to continue to enjoy popular support. Here we have a closed circle. Failure of the decision-making process is attributed to the lack of political will. But political will will neither develop nor translate into action in the absence of effective institutions. And the governments so far have found it impossible to develop such institutions.

Again, one turns to the Commission but finds the dice loaded against it. Rather than enhance the position of this crucial body, the member states jealously guard their power and authority. Furthermore, for years the Commission suffered the determined hostility of de Gaulle, continued in only slightly abated form by his successor. More recently, presumably on the conviction the Commission had been properly chastened, an atmosphere of indifference replaced the former animosity. Seeking some way of enhancing its status and gaining support from the member states, the Hallstein, Rey, Malfatti, Mansholt, and finally, the Ortoli Commissions experimented with practically every means—independence of and direct challenge to the governments, cooperation and docility, direct appeals to public opinion—to little avail.

The crisis of the Commission epitomizes the dilemma that the Europeans have neither solved nor squarely faced. The energy crisis and its frightening implications for Europe have dramatized the need for an effective Community—for the organization of resources, for the capacity to bring the Community's collective weight to bear internally and externally, for a Community with its own identity and the ability to speak with one voice. Yet the governments professing to want these results, notably France, cannot bring themselves to make the modest concessions of national sovereignty necessary to achieve the ends they each so tirelessly eulogize. In the galaxy of Community institutions a strong independent Commission is an indispensable element. However, even such determined supporters of the Community as the Dutch and the Germans display slight interest in the Commission. While the Commission suffers hostility, suspicion, or indifference at the political level of the member governments, it faces guerrilla attack from the national bureaucracies. Over the next few critical years, whatever the role of the Commission is to be, its functions as catalyst and Community leader must derive largely from its own efforts.

The European Community stage has been dominated by the Council of Ministers, occasional summit meetings, and the Commission. But the Community's prospects will continue to be substantially affected by two other institutions, the Court of Justice and the European Parliament.

The Court in Luxembourg receives scant attention, unfairly, since it has been an effective body. An independent court, adjudicating disputes arising from the existence of the Community and Community law, is vital to a Europe with federal ambitions. So far, the Court has escaped the greatest peril: the member states have not challenged its decisions, but have honored and enforced them.

The Parliament, an institution essential to political legitimacy, has two important missions: first, through its process of debate to open the Community to public view; second, closely related to the problem of effective Community operation and recovering the momentum of integration, to criticize, expose, cajole, and generate popular pressures to drive the Community toward action and decision.

For years Europe has been trapped in a medieval debate over legislative theology: Should the emphasis be on direct election of the European parliamentarians, or should the first step be to obtain additional power over legislation and especially money? The danger to the integration process is that energies will be exhausted on a chicken-or-the-egg argument: Which should come first—grabbing and exploiting implicit powers; or waiting, cap in hand, for new powers to be granted by governments or for direct elections? Europe seems ripe for a lively and independent Parliament with ideas of its own. By raising the indelicate question, publicizing the Community's deficiencies, and developing latent investigatory authority, the Parliament has the chance to become the gadfly of the entire integration movement.

The Member States

The principal actors on the European scene, as in 1950, remain the individual states. Thus any attempt to forecast the Community's prospects must probe the attitude of the member states toward it and, indeed, toward the idea of unity itself.

Europeans are wary of further complicating life by establishing yet another governmental level in Brussels. They struggle, as do Americans, with the distribution of governmental power—the problem of handing back to regional or local units, closer to the constituencies, power which has drifted to the top. In a world changing too rapidly, the known and established governmental structure offers a haven of security. The process of unification, while slow and obscure in its impact on the public, is nonetheless revolutionary. Pompidou exemplified the conservative instinct of seeking, consciously or unconsciously, to hold to the familiar patterns at a moment of profound social upheaval. In fact, for years the world seemed too much for Europe's leaders, all of whom lacked one or more of those qualities necessary to challenge the *status quo*—imagination, a firm domestic base, political power.

It can be argued that the running conflict and messy compromises between local and national interests and the broader community interest are part of the democratic process. This haphazard procedure, conducted within the framework and under the rules of a rudimentary Community constitution, is not the best or the worst, but probably the only, way to proceed. Among the ills of the clumsy system, however, is the fact that the sum of the efforts of national, vested interests is not necessarily the Community good. The preservation and the furthering of the larger Community interest require an awareness and self-conscious effort on the part of the national political leaders from the member states. A leader of the British Labour party, one of the minority deeply committed to Europe, readily acknowledged what should be done. But he went on to say privately that if he were openly to endorse a larger Community view of economic and social policy, even though it would be clearly in British interests, it would amount to political suicide because of his constituents' passions and short-term views.

The Community of nine is different qualitatively as well as quantitatively from the Community of six. The latter, during the fifteen years of Gaullism, tended to reduce contentious issues to a Franco-German confrontation. The danger in this process was French blackmail which degraded France, humiliated Germany, and left the other states impotent and frustrated. Cherishing their hard-won status as democratic partners, especially the precious rapprochement with France, German leaders dared not challenge charges of obstinacy or charges that espousal of opposing views were sinister echoes of the Third Reich, no matter how baseless. The enlarged Community changes the game and reduces the opportunity for this corrosive confrontation. With three rather than two major countries, the Community becomes an arena for shifting coalitions related to the changing patterns of member states' interests. A larger Community enhances the prospect of coalitions based on complementary national interests; not France pitted against the five and, ultimately, against the Germans.

A significant aspect of Community development has been the deep commitment of the smaller European countries to the process. In September 1972, when Norway voted to reject membership, one argument advanced had been that to enter the Community meant the end of Norwegian independence, of the Norwegian way of life. The original members of the Community had drawn a different conclusion. As they saw it, only by membership in a Community had they any chance to influence events, to express effectively a national point of view, and to preserve their national identity.

For the small countries, the Community is a means of containing Germany as well as of freeing them from prospective dominance by France or Germany, or both. The apprehension rooted in European history regarding the behavior of close neighbors has led the Benelux countries, the Netherlands especially, to look to England and to the United States for security. For these countries foreign policy might be seen as a series of linked concentric circles: European unity for intra-European political and economic reasons; the British in the Community in order to broaden and democratize the process; a Community of strong institutions weighted against easy dominance by the larger member states; an integrated Europe working with and not at cross-purposes with America; and a strong NATO. The smaller countries view uneasily the cosy practice of bilateral meetings between the French President, British Prime Minister, and German Chancellor. When accompanied by erosion of the power and decisiveness of Community institutions, the intimate understandings among the three leaders raise the ghost of big-power hegemony.

Although speaking for Britain, Sir Alec Douglas-Home made the case for the small countries. Home was responding to an attack by Enoch Powell, who had asserted that a Labour government outside the Common Market would be preferable to a Conservative government within it. As Powell rested his argument on the loss of sovereignty, Sir Alec insisted that those who use the word should be careful to understand what it means: "To my mind it means control over the future national destiny. By joining the Community we have achieved just that. Can anyone seriously suppose that the major powers of the world—the United States, Russia, China and Japan—would pay the close regard to our views if we were not a member of the Community? Our membership gives us an authority and an importance which we could never possibly achieve on our own, and we are already reaping the fruits of this fact."[4]

4. *The Sunday Times* (London), June 17, 1973.

Midstream in the painful "renegotiation" of British membership, with the majority of the parliamentary Labour party hostile to the Community, only a strenuous effort can recall the 1973 hopes and expectations of what the participation of England in Europe would mean. It seemed that Great Britain's membership in the Community could issue in a renaissance for both. British energy had been sapped by the human destruction of two wars. The end of the empire, the ugly situations in Rhodesia and South Africa, the war between Pakistan and India proved beyond doubt that the Commonwealth was not a vision of the future but a mirage. As the British arrived in Brussels in 1973, their optimism over the challenge of Europe startled their partners. In the mid-1960s Dean Acheson had infuriated many Britons with his aphorism that their country had lost an empire but not found a role. In 1973 their fascination with the European Community prompted some cynical Europeans to twist Acheson's phrase to read, "The British have lost a role but found an empire."

Many dedicated, weary, but still hopeful Europeans clung to the conviction that only the British could revive the integration movement. The record of the first year of British membership was ambiguous. It started well with the exceptionally high quality of British appointments to the Commission, the staff, and the British Permanent Delegation—objective evidence of Heath's commitment. Cabinet ministers and their staffs in general approached Community work constructively and well prepared. The British delegation attempted to stir up the European Parliament. The quality press in London took the Community seriously; the reporting was extensive and good. These were all hopeful signs. From the continental European vantage point, the British fitted into the Brussels machinery more easily than had been expected. The "old boys" were watching for any sign of a British take-over, but the most suspicious Europeans later gave credit to British rectitude.

1973 was not to be the year of British leadership. Heath's emphasis on relations with Paris and deference to Pompidou persisted beyond the point where this policy could be excused as a tactical imperative to successful negotiations. Those who had hoped for better things were to conclude that in Heath's latter months his approach to European affairs could only be described as "Gaullist." With the Yom Kippur war and energy crisis imposed on a country riven by internal political and economic strife, Heath might have played the Community card; but it would have been irrelevant. One year after entry, 31 percent in Britain thought membership good for the country, 34 percent thought it bad—judgments reached before the real effects of the oil and balance-of-payments crises had been felt. By early 1974 Heath's objective was survival. Indeed, caught in an economic vise, he eschewed a Community approach to the energy disaster, as advocated by Brandt, and cast his lot with the French and a policy of pure nationalism.

Those dreams of British leadership faded. Regardless of the spasmodic movements of British politics or the fortunes of the Wilson government, Europeans have come to view Great Britain as a liability, not an asset, certainly not as a "European" leader. North Sea oil has not altered the image of a polarized, inflation-ridden, economically stagnant society. It would take more than political magic to transform British antipathy to Europe into support. The process might have begun in 1973, but not in the face of Labour opposition. On the assumption that Britain remains in the Community, the most optimistic near-term prospects are for it to play a largely passive role, riding along with the tide, preoccupied with extracting whatever material benefits the Community offers. Over time, the subtle advantages of membership and growing network of relations should infuse British life, just as the anti-Europe Labour militants fear. Within this framework of a passive policy, carried out from a weak economic base, one may at least hope that the politicians will not prevent the skilled British civil service from making its unique contribution to Community development.

France, of course, lies at the center of the problems of the past and the hopes of the future. Living with France has been so difficult that Americans and Europeans frequently wondered if it would not be better to face the trials of life and the future without it. De Gaulle's unilateral action in 1966 driving NATO out of France and withdrawing France from the military side of the alliance seemed to force on the allies serious consideration of this option. During the worst of the Gaullist period, from the veto of British entry in 1963 until the General's departure in 1968, there was recurrent speculation that perhaps a Community without France but with Great Britain should be considered. No matter how attractive the non-French option, the realities of geography and Western culture have always driven reluctant partners back once again to the endless search for the secret of how to collaborate with the Gallic ally.

Here again, the perspective of two decades may be useful. After the difficulties of the Gaullist years there is a tendency to forget that behind postwar European-Atlantic achievements lie French inspiration, initiative, and leadership. The much maligned Fourth Republic, through Schuman, Monnet, and Hirsch, offered unity in lieu of the chaos of battered and drifting European states. Schuman's political courage and vision and Monnet's mastery of technique dominated the European scene. French leaders perceived the idea of a new Community as a means for dealing with the German problem, bringing Germany back into the family of law-abiding and democratic European nations, and as an equal.

As we now know, the relentless pressure which de Gaulle brought to bear on the integration process is perhaps less surprising than the fact that he tolerated it at all. The European Community embodied all that he detested. It was a hybrid political entity without legitimacy and with an obscure economic preoccupation. It was a Community rooted in the idea of equality rather than an alliance of states in which the strongest and most assertive would dominate. It was a Europe united in order to work in partnership with the United States instead of a Europe strong enough to free itself from a degrading dependence on that uncultured, polyglot nation across the Atlantic. Because of his convictions, his exceptional will, and political skill, de Gaulle's threats, no matter how grotesque, were always credible. For ten years he held the Community hostage. His move against NATO had made the menace real. De Gaulle's confidence and histrionics half convinced many observers that he might just be able to square the circle: there could be a European Europe without institutions, an aggregation of sovereign states —led by France. France was not strong, and he knew it. Yet he persuaded the world to accept not what existed but what he asserted. He dreamed of a Europe so powerful that it could recover its rightful mission as world leader, able to meet both America and the Soviet Union on equal terms. As Francis Bacon would say, de Gaulle's dilemma was to wish for the result but to be unable to bear the means.

The decade 1958 to 1968 is still too close for mature evaluation. But one effect of Gaullist domination was concentration by France's partners on simple survival of the Community. On the positive side there was cautious, limited movement, especially with regard to tasks explicitly required by the treaty. The agriculture program was initiated, of obvious benefit to France; to a degree it reversed the situation and held de Gaulle hostage to the Community. The Kennedy Round of tariff negotiations was brought to a successful conclusion.

As important as the Gaullist period was its legacy. Pompidou's objectives and European diplomacy were obscure. While de Gaulle was dogmatic, Pompidou was pragmatic, and certainly more realistic than his predecessor. Where the General was contemptuous of the bureaucracy, Pompidou was suspicious. It was hard to determine whether French obstructionism in Brussels was in response to Pompidou's instructions, or rather a continuance of Gaullist momentum which Pompidou lacked the interest or the will to challenge. The fact of the matter is that the French bureaucracy continued to pursue policies and tactics almost identical to those of the Gaullist period. The situation baffled France's partners who had hoped and expected that, after the March 1973 elections, Pompidou would become his own man, free to engage in a more flexible and realistic European policy. In his bilateral and summit conferences he displayed a pliancy and willingness to join with his colleagues in major Community decisions, frequently overruling his advisers. Yet these decisions were negated or ignored by these same French subordinates when the moment came for execution in Brussels. The question remains: Was it bureaucracy out of control or, more likely, a French Byzantium? Whatever the goals and the tactical deviousness of Pompidou, the situation was different from that of the Gaullist period. The shift in French leadership made British entry into the Community possible.

Pompidou's death and the elections of May 1974 allowed Giscard d'Estaing to engineer the end of Gaullism. His convictions about Europe were refreshing. In 1969 when he was not in office, Giscard visited Brussels for discussions with the Commission. At the time he said, "Modern independence is defined by size. A size for independence exists today, a point from which a country can act in the world context. It is thus that in the monetary field or in the field of defense, the isolated European countries have not been able to act. . . . In the world in which we live, it is within the framework of the European institutions that our countries can best exercise together their sovereignty and safeguard the modern form of their independence."[5] Pursuit of such a policy depended on the new French President's capacity to cope with an imposing array

5. *Europe*, Agence Internationale d'Information pour la Presse, May 31, 1974.

of internal issues—a sharply divided country, deep-seated economic and social problems, an entrenched Gaullist bureaucracy. After the years of de Gaulle and Pompidou it was uncertain whether the earlier, brilliantly constructive period of 1950 to 1958 was the real France or an aberration. The performance of the Giscard government would provide the answer.

Much depends, too, on how Germany plays its role. Its stake in European unity is unique. Since the days of Adenauer, German leaders have looked upon the Community as the essential framework for their country's development, one which would permit Germany to prosper without reviving the fears of its neighbors. Perceptive Germans have also seen the organic Community ties as an inhibition against men of the future who might be tempted by Western division and failure to set German foreign policy on an entirely different course. *Ostpolitik* demonstrated the pull of the East on Germany and the strength of the old illusion that Germany has a special mission as bridge between East and West.

German leaders who fought for European integration wondered at the stubborn obtuseness of the French in weakening the Community and draining it of content. The departure of de Gaulle freed the Federal Republic to play a more active and forceful role in Community development. German elections in the spring of 1973 gave evidence of the strength of the democratic process. The major lines of *Ostpolitik* had been established and ratified. The question was whether Brandt would act and how. Despite the logical imperatives of Germany's commitment to the Community and the consistent support of political leaders and political parties, Bonn could not bring itself to become the inspirer and leader of the integration process. Among his contemporaries Brandt had emerged as the outstanding statesman, the symbol of integrity; yet his was an elusive quality. The decisive pursuit of announced policy was lacking; the result of the oratory was an echo. The bloom of Brandt's Eastern policy was quickly gone. Internal discontent over economic and social problems was rising, and dissension was fracturing his Social Democratic Party. A spy in his personal cabinet was only the fatal, last straw that precipitated his resignation of office.

Brandt's departure completed the political transformation of Western Europe. The transition to Helmut Schmidt demonstrated the strength of German democracy. But the political emphasis would be different. His biases were domestic rather than foreign, his interests more Atlantic than European. His nationalism was certainly more in tune with the mood of young SPD politicians, men indifferent to European integration and whose goals did not exceed the attainment of political power. Egon Bahr, Brandt's able if notorious associate, expressed a view not uncongenial with this group, and with some young Christian Democrat politicians as well. Bahr said that if it came to a choice between the European Community and Germany, he would choose the latter.[6]

The year 1974 swept away the leading political figures and saw them replaced by men with different policies and styles. Curiously, the new political alignments suggested the past more than anything. Again, if Europe were to progress, it would be on the basis of Franco-German collaboration, with Britain once more on the sidelines.

6. Walter Hahn, *Orbis*, Vol. XVI (Winter 1973).

Chapter III

The United States and a United Europe (1945-1969)

Beyond the normal difficulties of adducing American attitudes on involved foreign issues there is the special problem of sorting out the constant factors from the frenetic moods of the moment. Certainly, extensive changes have occurred in America's perception of the world and of Europe, but the questions are to what degree, in what areas, and are they permanent or subject to modification?

The constraints surrounding any American foreign policy with respect to an evolving European union are extensive. Public moods, Congressional attitudes, popular myths, the convictions of interest groups—all place limits on the real diplomatic world. In a complex interplay, these general factors affect the capacity and will of the executive to lead and, conversely, the President and his aides contribute to the very attitudes that restrict the executive's field of action. It is equally obvious that American opinion, to the extent that it exists at all, is influenced by the progress of European union, the actions of the Community, and the availability of information—or misinformation. Unless both European and American constraints are identified and accommodated, drawing up possible lines of American policy becomes nothing more than an academic exercise.

It has been a quite natural and well-established American conviction that unification would offer the old continent some of the advantages which a federal system is thought to have bestowed on the new: the benefits of continental scale, nearly essential, it seems, in this advanced industrial age; and a political system which has successfully woven together diverse European peoples. To embrace this idea is not a new, twentieth-century fixation. Immediately after the Philadelphia convention

Benjamin Franklin extolled to French friends the virtues of the new constitution and urged that Europe consider some similar political structure.

Marshall Plan, Schuman Plan, and an Alternative Vision

World War II and the Marshall Plan—and the still vivid memory of the first World War—gave focus and thrust to a policy of support for European unity. Drawn against its will into a global conflict, America emerged convinced that there were no problems energetic effort could not solve, particularly if reinforced with money. Stalin, in sweeping aside the wartime collaboration, exposed the power vacuum in Western Europe and gave the issue an additional dimension and sharp urgency. Officials in the field, the executive branch, and the Congress were caught up in the enthusiasm of a great common endeavor which imbued the country. Despite the Herculean task of European recovery, Americans eagerly looked beyond the restoration of economies to a different Europe. Thus, out of the spirit of the Marshall Plan and the dialogue between the executive and the legislature incidental to the authorization and appropriation process, Congress came almost routinely to urge the merit of European unity.

As the immediate problems of postwar Europe were primarily economic, economists and an economic bias dominated reconstruction planning. Nothing could be more natural than that these confident officials, unburdened by the diplomatic baggage of what could not be done, should see the key to Europe's problems within a single concept, "economy of scale." The genius of the Marshall Plan had been to approach the problem as a whole and to reject the first European reaction. The potential recipients had argued for a series of bilateral programs; Washington replied by imposing on the Europeans the responsibility of planning a comprehensive approach. The institution created to meet this demand, the Organization for European Economic Cooperation (OEEC), laid the base of experience and intellectual conditioning for the Schuman Plan. Monnet's unique role in World War I, during the interwar period, in World War II procurement, and then in postwar recovery made it natural that he should turn to economic means as the way to achieve political ends. Furthermore, the demanding economic problems of Europe and the uninhibited thinking of economists opened up all issues for examination, including those which were essentially political.

Two world wars born of the European nation-state system hardened American judgment as to the iniquities of European nationalism and the need for a new European structure if peace were to be secured. The United States was intellectually ready for a novel approach. Schuman's initiative, which was to prepare a place for Germany within Western Europe, coincided with Acheson's search for political means of bringing Germany into the Atlantic system. Nonetheless, Schuman's timing and the concentration on coal and steel caught Washington off guard. It was not an idea which fitted easily into the traditional thought patterns of governments. And as soon as one moved beyond the simple, grand goals of Schuman's proposal, matters became complicated. The political objectives faded behind a maze of economic detail. Officials whose concerns and interests were largely politics and security found themselves forced to work with—or worse, to understand—experts whose business was economics. After twenty years this problem of communication between the political and economic cultures remains largely unresolved. In view of the Plan's economic trappings, it was inevitable that some economic experts thought they detected no more than a revival of the classical European cartel in modern dress. Nevertheless, thanks to the mood of experimentation and the vivid memory of the disastrous results of European nationalism, American support was quick and firm.

In analysis of the early momentum for European unity there has been no agreement on the importance of the contribution made by the Cold War and Stalin. For those who lived through the period it is hard to follow the insistence of revisionist historians that in the critical postwar years the Soviet Union was not expansionist, that it posed no military threat, and that the abusive language was merely reaction to Western provocation and hostility. It is sufficient to note that every responsible American or European leader at that time believed the threat was real. The American nuclear monopoly limited for the moment the risk of Soviet military moves; but Europeans and Americans were convinced that the Soviet Union would exploit any points of Western weakness. By 1950 the Russians had consolidated their hold on Eastern Europe. In contrast, the United States worried about a still destitute Western Europe which, weak and fragmented, could only be a constant temptation to the Soviets. America considered an economically strong and united Western Europe indispensable against both pressure or attack from the East.

On any major program or line of policy each supporter attaches different weight to different factors. For some Europeans and Americans, the anti-Communist argument was decisive; for others, the goal of a strong and coherent Western Europe was the chief objective. The latter view included, of course, the idea that a united Europe would be better able to counter Soviet influence and, beyond that, exert a powerful attraction to the captive nations of Eastern Europe. In the event, European and American conviction that the Soviet Union menaced Western Europe was unquestionably a significant factor in bringing the Community into being and gaining American support.

From the outset the idea of European union stimulated resistance among those who dreamed of a quite different Atlantic and world order. European union ran counter to the vision of the globalists, the federalists, and the economic multilateralists. For those whose goal was an "Atlantic Community," blossoming naturally from the seeds of the OEEC and NATO, the Schuman Plan and talk of European union were heresy. In the early years, the conflict generated in Washington by these alternative concepts was real. America's surge of postwar internationalism released itself in supporting the United Nations and, among influential special interests, the multilateral economic system. The exceptions and rationalizations required to fit an embryonic European union into this policy framework were discomforting. And there was a running battle with those who regarded NATO as the flywheel of European policy. They were in a strong position. The semiannual ministerial meetings assured the high-level interest engendered by the daily discussions of the NATO Council in permanent session. Although European economic union was peripheral to NATO and quite separate from the mission of the Organization for Economic Cooperation and Development (OECD) as it evolved from the OEEC, the concept disturbed the fraternal harmony of these more traditional international organizations.

Another factor was British foreign policy. For a decade Britain's self-exclusion from the European Community complicated American policy-making. As a part of its strategy of indifference and then hostility to European union, Great Britain eulogized Atlantic arrangements. The skill of British diplomacy and easy intimacy of American and British officials and legislators gave the Atlantic Community alternative a synthetic validity. In time, however, the continued progress of the Community and Macmillan's reversal of British policy reduced the notion of an Atlantic Community to the status of emotive political rhetoric.

Despite its limited cachet the concept of an Atlantic Community could not be entirely dismissed. Paradoxically, the more the European Community succeeded, the more questions it raised about the viability of the multilateral economic system. In complex ways European union, nationalism, and an Atlantic Community were bound together. One device for resisting the transfer of power implicit in European union was to advance an Atlantic alternative in the knowledge that the basic ingredient of any Atlantic Community had to be the sovereign nation-state. And finally, for the United States, the Atlantic option always appealed to those whose taste runs to horse and rabbit stew—one oversized American horse and fourteen European rabbits.

America and the Developing European Community

After Schuman's proposal of a European Coal and Steel Community in May 1950, Jean Monnet had to flesh out the bare bones of the concept. Consistent with Monnet's special techniques for drawing on advice from whatever source, he in effect made William Tomlinson, the Treasury attaché at the American Embassy in Paris, an unofficial member of his staff. American officers and experts worked interchangeably with Monnet's European aides. In subsequent years, as Europe progressed, such intimacy naturally declined. But as late as the 1960s, close, informal collaboration between Americans and Europeans was the rule. By the 1970s it was the rare exception.

Although Europeans were leading, inspiring, and forcing the pace of European policy, they welcomed and expected political and technical assistance from the United States. Such give-and-take was so natural that the utter contrast with the present requires a second look at earlier practice. It is fashionable these days to think of that period as one of patron-client relations, of an overbearing America. The Europeans did not see it that way. The Americans most closely involved were deeply committed to the concept of European unity, were fascinated with the process; they fraternized but did not patronize. The nature of this co-operation has been obscured when drawn into the controversy within Europe between the advocates and the opponents of European union.

The latter, of course, resented any American action which gave comfort to what they were against. The reaction was similar among Americans who questioned government policy. They complained of the excessive commitment of the various Washington administrations, of America's becoming far too involved.

The intimacy and the assumption of close American-European relations during the 1950s and early 1960s can be seen in the resolutions of the Action Committee for a United States of Europe. At that time the Action Committee, with its membership of political party leaders and trade unionists, was the planning staff, lobbyist, and consensus-builder of European unity. Repeatedly, the Committee proposed a Comité d'Entente as a mechanism for the European Community and the United States to deal with one another on a systematic and equal basis. President Kennedy's call in 1962 for an Atlantic Partnership rested on the identical premise of continuing and close relations between America and a unified Europe. Monnet quickly endorsed the principle of an "equal partnership." There was little questioning of this grand design on either side of the Atlantic. Partnership as a goal was not in dispute; it was only a matter of whether the Europeans could make sufficient progress to convert the objective of partnership into reality. Dean Acheson, who endorsed both European unity and the general goals of partnership, nonetheless gagged on the adjective "equal"; his experience as a lawyer led him to insist that he had seen and been engaged in many partnerships, but never one that was equal.

In 1962, despite storm warnings from de Gaulle, the general Atlantic mood was optimistic, with attention directed to avoiding hazards in the way rather than questioning whether it was the right one—or whether America and Europe should both be on the same road. For the next few miles the route was clear, including the obstacles. At some vague, distant point lay the shimmering, undefined goal of partnership. There was no agreement, either in America or Europe, on the critical middle stages— the optimists could use as their text Cromwell's saying, "No man goes farther than the man who doesn't know where he is going." The pessimists could lean on Sararoza, the Spanish cynic, who observed, "I don't know where we are going. All I know is that wherever it may be we shall lose our way."

American euphoria was broken, in 1963, by the French veto of the British negotiations. Washington watched with increasing discourage-

ment as Europe, instead of progressing toward unity which was fundamental to the partnership policy, turned to debilitating, internal conflict.
Gaullism would in one way or another dominate the European scene for
the rest of the decade. The other members of the Community were
severely disadvantaged in their confrontation with de Gaulle. Decisions
among them on the responses to challenges from Paris had to be threshed
out first within each national cabinet and then negotiated with the
other governments. The difficulties in arriving at a single position were
formidable. De Gaulle's motives and strategy were obscure, but his
tactics brilliant. Although the other five nations were as one in their
condemnation of French policy, each had its own notion of what the
General was up to and how best to meet the problem. As it was a highly
subjective process, ultimate decisions among the five were generally
poor compromises, always painfully reached. Frequently, by the time the
five finally made up their collective mind, de Gaulle had shifted his
ground or altered his demands.

The decade of the 1960s was a period of dramatic change in the relative economic status of Europe and the United States. Dollars moved
from scarcity to glut; Europe's chronic balance-of-payments deficits
moved to surpluses. By the late 1960s inflation loomed as the great,
unmanageable issue. A European economy of abundance produced an
atmosphere of complacency. The luster of long-term goals faded in the
glow of short-term consumer satisfaction. Among the politicians who
were sensitive to the changed situation, few were daring enough to
advocate national concessions for some future European good.

In this period of social and economic upheaval and intense internal
bargaining, Europe assumed that the benign support of America, well
outside the chaos of change, was as solid as ever. In December 1968,
during his last visit to Brussels before leaving office, Secretary Rusk met
with the European Commission. In his valedictory statement he warned
of the dangers in European complacency, "You pay us a great com-
pliment by taking the United States for granted." His warning was
prescient. There was an unreal quality to this period. Great changes were
taking place—within Europe, in standards of living, between Europe
and the United States—but it was almost as though no one could bring
himself to recognize the changes and draw the appropriate conclusions.
There seemed to be an unspoken belief that reiterated litanies about past
policies would somehow invest them with new vitality.

During the last half of the 1960s the Kennedy Round trade negotiations were the major factor in relations between the Community and the United States. The process began with Congressional consideration and enactment of the Trade Expansion Act of 1962 and ended when the negotiations were brought to a successful conclusion in the fall of 1968. President Kennedy would never have sought such far-reaching authority from the Congress had British entry into an expanded Community not been in prospect. Just as the fact of the European Community produced the Kennedy Round, so, in the final analysis, success or failure could be determined by negotiations between the United States and the Community.

It is remarkable that such long, difficult, pugnacious negotiations did not lead to real damage to American-European relations. Trade negotiations are adversary proceedings. Negotiators on each side were skilled and tenacious. Yet the Atlantic framework was sufficiently strong to absorb the shocks of the extended affair. Moreover, the Community proved itself by showing that it could organize difficult negotiations and bring them to a successful conclusion. In reviewing the Kennedy Round well after the event, Eric Wyndham-White, then Director-General of GATT who had great respect for the American negotiators Christian Herter, William Roth, and Michael Blumenthal, said that if he were asked to name one man who deserved credit for the ultimate success he would nominate Jean Rey. This was not merely a tribute to Rey's negotiating skill, but more importantly to his leadership within the Community, his willingness to take courageous positions and then force the member governments to support him.

While relations between Europe and the United States were not adversely affected by the negotiating battles, in a subtle way general American attitudes toward the Community were conditioned by them. For five years America's awareness of the Community was tied to the drama of crises arising out of trade bargaining. The friction of these negotiations became the core of the new American view of the Community as a hard bargainer, an adversary.

The long shadow of de Gaulle falls across this confused scene. The premise of the early 1950s that a united Europe and the United States would in the very nature of things work together was replaced by misgiving that the European Community would be subjected to France and French policies. There was more to this than the professional anti-

Gaullism of some Washington officials. The Europe de Gaulle envisioned, the Europe embraced by his followers, had to be self-consciously at odds with the United States; indeed, its personality took shape from its very separateness.

A Gaullist European Community was a prospect which corresponded nicely to the suspicions of the domestic agencies in Washington. The reverence of the French for gold as the center of the monetary system, their tenacious support of every aspect of the Common Agricultural Policy, their advocacy of regional and reverse preferences, their stubborn resistance in the 1960s to European currency revaluations and new trade negotiations were held up as evidence of what could be expected from a French-controlled Community. Even if the French could not impose their views, they could paralyze the Community. The American business community shared much of this prognosis.

The faltering of Europe, beset by a run of bad luck, further undercut American support. Americans were discouraged by recurrent internal Community crises over agriculture, finance and institutions, by the twice aborted British negotiation, by European energies exhausted by insistent domestic demands, by the absence of any European leader ready to lead the "European" movement. While de Gaulle was in power, no case could be made for an active European policy on the part of the United States. But even after his departure the confusion of Europe was such that an advocate of the European Community was hard put to describe just what America might do.

The Erosion of American Support

The original rationale for American support of European unity is easier to identify and explain than the ambiguous erosion of this commitment.

American disenchantment with the Community became a product of our disillusioned rejection of all large conceptions, a part of the general mood of pessimism. As promises of the postwar period were shown to be illusory, the country came to doubt many old articles of faith. The United Nations turned out to be only another forum for empty verbal conflict rather than a system which would carry forward wartime co-operation. Critics charged that the trade-and-payments system had come to benefit almost everyone but the United States; the array of imaginative economic programs from Point Four technical assistance to development aid left unchanged the disparities between rich and poor, while military juntas tightened their grip and democracy was in retreat everywhere.

By the mid-1960s domestic issues were major contributors to national pessimism. Foreign affairs did little to relieve the gloom. Yet, apart from Vietnam, these matters were not central to the worries of Americans. The collapse of faith in simple solutions to complex problems abroad coincided with increased sensitivity to the range of domestic ills which had either been ignored or dealt with inadequately. Finally, America lost its confidence in the miraculous properties of initiative, energy, money—and in the conviction of a divine preference for Americans and His loyal assistance to their enterprises.

By the end of the decade the onslaught of foreign economic problems was real, extensive, and frightening. Americans reeled under the psychological shock of a fall from grace—from chronic surpluses to massive deficits, from an impregnable dollar to inconvertibility. The reversal of fortune was so abrupt and complete that the causes and implications could neither be comprehended nor absorbed. Initial reactions were fear and resentment.

From the beginning the idea of European union encompassed both economic and political factors. Europeans and Americans were not precise about the interrelationship and how political union would come about. There was a strong element of faith, a sense of inevitability about political union, which gave the process a special aura. What seemed the tide of history in 1950 became dubious in 1970. Europeans talked more of political unity, and disagreed more on what it was and how to reach it. European confusion and doubt discouraged those Americans whose support depended on a natural progression from economics to politics. And when the political ideal was missing, the results of greater economic unity seemed more menacing than promising. Those who had questioned the policy from the outset were armed for battle. They threw back at supporters the old argument, "The United States is prepared to pay some economic price for European political unity." The critics asked, "What political unity?" Furthermore, as a good friend of the Community, Deputy Undersecretary Nathaniel Samuels put it, in view of the economic strength of the European Community and the trade and financial plight of the United States, why should America be asked to pay any economic price at all?

A further adverse development was the disappearance from the governmental scene of the American "Europeans." This group included career officers and transients in government from private life. Some, like David Bruce, had come during the war and stayed; others, like George Ball, had left at the end of the postwar period and were to return. It was a loosely knit group, allied in its support of European union, sensitive to Europe's objectives and problems, and tied by close friendship to the Europeans involved. Knowledge and personal relationships created an atmosphere conducive to constructive Atlantic collaboration in the public interest. The spirit was analogous to that of the war: a joint effort to solve common problems. Obviously there were European or American interests to be protected and issues to be negotiated, but they were somehow secondary. It was believed that a general atmosphere of intimate cooperation could only facilitate the resolution of such issues. This unexpected wartime legacy of personal relationships lubricated Atlantic relations. Some saw it as a microcosm of how an Atlantic partnership might work.

Washington's lack of "Europeans" can be attributed to several factors. By 1970, World War II was a quarter of a century into history. The postwar ferment and challenge had been lost in a new world and a new situation. It was inevitable that many career officers and others from the private world would have departed. The new generation of governmental officials had had none of this commitment. As for the transients, there was a sharp difference between Democratic and Republican administrations. The former tended to attract people who were drawn to government as a vocation while the Republican party, with its business orientation, brought to Washington men who regarded government service as a public duty but still a detour from their chosen careers.

As the Johnson administration decayed, so did the practice of intimate, continuous dialogue at all levels between Europeans and Americans. Jean Monnet had had easy access to Eisenhower and Dulles and then to Kennedy. At the state reception following Kennedy's funeral Monnet was the only nonofficial guest to be invited by President Johnson. This was to be Monnet's last visit to Washington. Kurt Birrenbach, that remarkable German businessman-statesman, normally met several times each year with Kennedy, McGeorge Bundy, and Dean Acheson. These and other Europeans searched with mounting despair for those officials with whom they could talk informally and candidly, as they had in the past with both Democratic and Republican administrations. By the 1970s they were driven to sharing frustrations with the Eastern establishment outcasts at wistful meetings of the Council on Foreign Relations. The new European generation, less interested in any event, was discouraged from attempting to revive the dialogue.

Chapter IV

The Nixon Years

Aside from successfully resisting Congressional efforts to reduce the number of American forces in Europe unilaterally, the Nixon administration in its first term gave scant attention to relations with Western Europe. The demands of Peking, Moscow, and Vietnam were such that neither Nixon nor Kissinger had much time for other pursuits. Furthermore, as we have seen, from 1969 to 1973 the European scene was one of confusion and transition. The "Nixon Doctrine" had the not insignificant virtue of accepting the obvious: the decline of America's relative power and national will; its fatigue with world leadership; and, in the case of Europe, recognition of the increasing desire of the Europeans to manage their own affairs. But it was applied to the Community as a further excuse for inaction. Washington insisted that the United States would cease intruding into internal European affairs, attempting to dictate the shape of Europe, repeating past errors where the enthusiasm for European unity had allegedly exceeded that of the Europeans—and, not least, that of the French. From another perspective the White House "cease and desist" order was part of the traditional political minuet in which each new administration insists it is doing something strikingly different from the administration it has replaced.

So much of this analysis is critical of the Nixon administration that I should like to insert a few personal references. Among the extraordinary revelations of Watergate emerged Nixon's paranoiac conviction that he had inherited a government of partisan enemies. It showed a shocking cynicism about the public servants. After some three decades of association with the federal bureaucracy, my conclusion is that the people who select careers in government are eager to serve loyally whatever administration has been elected to power. If, however, the bureaucracy is held in suspicion and kept in ignorance, inevitably it will act in ways that seem to confirm the dark expectations of the White House.

While I could not erase from memory Nixon's campaigns against Jerry Voorhees and Helen Douglas and his association with McCarthyism, I was ready to believe that the man would rise to the job. When Senator Brooke came to Brussels in late 1968 and told of conversations with Nixon, of the latter's commitment to European unity, I was hopeful. Subsequently and by sheer chance I was in Washington immediately after the inauguration. As a result of a courtesy call on Secretary Rogers, he insisted, over Kissinger's objections, that I do the briefing on the European Community for Nixon in preparation for his European trip in February 1969. Previously, I had had limited experience in presenting background information to Presidents Kennedy and Johnson. Nixon's close attention, knowledge of the field, and intelligent questioning set him off as a distinctly superior interlocutor. I returned to Brussels persuaded that Brooke was right and, furthermore, ready to subscribe to that popular belief that we were in the presence of a "new Nixon." For a moment it seemed that a renaissance in American-Community relations was possible.

On the contrary, for the next four years it was difficult to detect any coherent pattern in American policy toward Europe. In earlier periods the State Department, backed by the White House, constantly sought—with mixed results—to aid the Community in its painful process of institutional development. Without illusion about the real authority or power of the European Commission, past administrations worked with the Commission and tried to enhance its status. The reverse was true during the first Nixon term. In fact, Washington searched for some alternative approach, for ways of by-passing the Commission and of dealing directly with the member governments. There was no doubt that whenever Washington had serious business to transact, it would be done with France, Britain, and Germany, in that order. As for policy toward the Community, the formal words came out right but they hardly corresponded with American action.

The United States seemed to be running a modern, split-level foreign policy. The White House press office issued, under State Department prodding, periodic pronouncements of support for European unity while

Cabinet officers and "sources close to the President" talked "tough" and muttered of trade war. American intentions, however, seemed all too clear: continuing, undiscriminating pressure on trade and agricultural issues, some of which were real, others advanced in order to display zeal in the executive branch. The unease and complaints of Europeans grew as they tried to reconcile America's actions with America's words, one result of which was to prompt vigorous assertion by Washington of lofty purpose and unchanged policy. We were well on our way to adding another problem to Atlantic relations; Europeans ceased believing what they were told. By 1973 many of them were convinced that it was no longer American policy to support European unity.

Senator John Kennedy once quoted some advice by Liddell Hart in an article discussing American relations with enemies, "Keep strong, if possible. In any case, keep cool. Have unlimited patience. Never corner an opponent, and always assist him to save face. Put yourself in his shoes so as to see things through his eyes. Avoid self-righteousness like the devil. Nothing is so self-blinding."[1] We can see how far we have come by noting the pertinence of these maxims to our relations with our allies—and the extent to which they have been ignored.

In domestic terms the split-level approach to foreign relations can be shrewd politics, in offering a smorgasbord of policies. There was soft language for the Atlantic do-gooders; sharp criticism of Europe for the irate Congressman or the textile mill owner in South Carolina. But it was not foreign policy.

The Formative Biases

No one familiar with Nixon's or Kissinger's commitment to bilateral diplomacy expected the new administration to be much interested in the European Community. The bearish forecast rested as well on their obvious fascination with de Gaulle. The President's captivation transcended calculations of how to manage relations with the French. Rather, de Gaulle cast a personal spell. This was what a political leader should be—remote, princely in comportment, pragmatic, master of surprise, manager of men and situations, unmoved by public opinion, and aloof from the legislative process. An early Presidential hyperbole commemorated the General as "the greatest leader of our time."

1. *Saturday Review of Literature*, Sept. 3, 1960.

Nixon, while out of office, experienced the flattery of reception by de Gaulle. As President, his admiration and obligation led easily to the conviction that his predecessors had never understood de Gaulle and, furthermore, had hopelessly bungled relations with France. As France was at the heart of American relations—and problems—with Western Europe, then priority would be given to American–French relations as the key to the solution of the larger Western European issues. An additional justification for deference to Paris was the desire of the administration to engage French assistance, and minimize potential French opposition, with regard to Vietnam. American policy was to accept France as the spokesman for Europe, to flatter the French, to search constantly for areas susceptible to special American–French cooperation, and, of course, to avoid crossing French interests. In short, the French connection was assiduously cultivated. Pompidou inherited intact the special American attention that had been lavished on de Gaulle.

Any doubts about the seriousness of the new administration's tactical approach to Europe were dispelled in the early weeks of 1969. When the President's first trip to Europe was planned, it was touch-and-go whether during his Brussels stopover he would even meet with the European Commission. His schedule included travel out to the NATO headquarters for extensive discussion with the Council and the Secretary General, a call on Belgian officials, and a luncheon given by the King. Grudgingly, the Commission was invited to an audience with Nixon at his suite at the Hilton, despite the fact that the Commission headquarters were less than five minutes from his hotel. The private justification for this off-hand treatment was to avoid offending the French. Nixon and Kissinger were keenly aware of de Gaulle's hostility to the political pretensions of the Commission and were more anxious to avoid offending French sensibilities than to establish a relationship with the Community.

As the conduct of American foreign affairs came to rest exclusively in the hands of two men, Kissinger's attitudes were a critical factor. The whole idea of European integration was sharply at odds with his approach to international affairs. His earlier, professorial conclusions about nineteenth-century diplomacy stuck in the minds of European officials. What greater folly than for the major power to assist in the organization of what could become an independent coalition of otherwise subordinate European states? What could be more alien to this philosophy of foreign affairs than the hybrid, pre-federal structure being built in Brussels out of economic materials? Contributing to this bias were Kissinger's ignorance of economics, shared by Nixon, and their common interest in avoiding the subject. Kissinger's personal weakness in this area could have been at least partially offset if, during his last several years in the White House, he had held on to foreign economic policy and assigned a strong deputy to that field. Instead, he consented to a transfer of the function from his office and the appointment of a separate assistant to the President charged with international economic affairs. He was to regret it. Kissinger's predecessors, who never doubted the integral relationship between national security and economics, had not made this error.

Even NATO, despite the Nixon administration's commitment to the organization, was ignored on critical issues. From the initial shock of the Moscow visit in 1972, the alliance suffered faulty and delayed briefings on American intentions and actions. Furthermore, as the vitality of NATO depends heavily on the American Permanent Representative, the interregnum after Ambassador Ellsworth's departure in mid-1971 raised doubts in European minds about the seriousness of American support of NATO. Nine months elapsed before David Kennedy was finally appointed to replace Ellsworth. To the dismay of his colleagues on the Council he addressed himself not to the alliance but to extensive, irrelevant negotiations with the Spaniards, Italians, and Japanese regarding voluntary restriction of shoe and textile exports to the United States. American press comment in 1973 was not helpful to Kennedy's successor, Donald Rumsfeld, suggesting on his arrival in Brussels that the NATO assignment was an educational experience and a stepping stone to the Illinois senatorial race.

Occasional activity regarding Western Europe was predominantly secretive and bilateral. For years Kissinger would return from Moscow by way of Paris, Bonn, and London, with the latter two capitals thrown in largely to provide cover for the visit to France. Although he discussed matters of critical concern to NATO, he neglected to add NATO headquarters to his itinerary. The secret briefings by the U.S. Mission to the NATO Council were less revealing than those Kissinger would subsequently give to the White House correspondents. Nonetheless, Ambassador Rumsfeld gained the regard of his colleagues who generously forgave the thinness of his briefing, aware that he could not inform the

Council of what Washington failed or was determined not to tell him. Washington's obsession with national diplomacy made it exceedingly difficult for the European governments to break away from bilateral habits which were at odds with their expressed Community commitments.

Further Estrangement

After the Kennedy Round, no major business drew the Community and the United States into common endeavors. The five and the French settled down to their internal, doctrinal dispute about the ultimate construction of Europe. By 1970 the United States was sinking even more deeply into the quagmire of Vietnam, while a new sharpness crept into its own internal debate on domestic issues.

Europeans and Americans had abundant excuses for setting aside Atlantic relations, at least for the moment. Almost with relief, Europe turned away from an America it didn't know to concentrate on the British negotiations as the urgent business at hand. Europeans refused to face the slow but steady deterioration in European-American relations. The problem, they insisted, was basically due to the internal European stalemate. Once the British were in and Europe again began to move, "the American problem" would automatically right itself. It was a convenient rationalization.

The mutual indifference and complacency between America and the Community at the turn of the decade began to be replaced by increasing incompatibility. In earlier periods the emphasis in European and American relations was cooperation, with contention present but clearly subordinate. By 1970 the emphasis was reversed. For America everything was tested for its effect on the balance of payments. Rather than attempt to understand America's difficult position, the Europeans were more inclined to debate the matter; especially to prove, no matter the issue, that the blame could not be placed on Europe. This was an awkward brief to argue as controversy swelled with regard to NATO burden-sharing and the balance-of-payments offset negotiations. Apparent inequities which the United States had earlier been reluctantly willing to live with were no longer acceptable under pressure of the payments deficit.

Attention focused on trade issues, especially agriculture. The Common Agriculture Policy, which until 1970 had been a prospective menace, began to have specific, adverse effects on American exports. For a few crops—but important ones such as wheat and feed grains—the agricultural levy system turned out to be quite as restrictive as had been anticipated. Furthermore, as the Nixon administration concentrated on the critical farm vote in the 1970 elections, Washington's aversion to the Community's agricultural policies became an obsession. Mediterranean preferences were also no longer a theoretical issue debated among trade policy experts, but a matter of specific Community restrictions which harmed a well-organized and noisy American interest group—the California and Arizona citrus growers.

The storm broke on August 15, 1971, wreaking havoc on the international monetary system. America was no longer above world financial battles; at the crucial moment America had acted without prior consultation. There was, nonetheless, a considerable degree of European understanding, even a certain admiration for the administration's break with the past. The Europeans agreed in general with the monetary measures. Their resentment was aroused by the tariff surtax but centered on Washington's demands for unilateral trade concessions. They only dimly recognized that they were witnessing the end of an economic era.

American maneuvering with Peking and Moscow and the continuing war in Vietnam increased the Europeans' perplexity about Washington's foreign policy. The European reaction to Vietnam was similar to that of the American people; after a time a passion could no longer be sustained. So, without support or approval of American actions or policy, the sharpness of official criticism declined. The Christmas bombing in 1972, however, brought a change. For the first time Europeans who had consistently sought to understand American policies in Southeast Asia and had attempted to explain them to fellow Europeans reacted with passion and sorrow. When Alastair Buchan, Jean Rey, and Bertrand de Jouvenel openly criticized the administration, the magnitude of the disaffection became apparent. Washington hoped that the bombing would be forgotten in the euphoria of the uneasy peace which followed. That Europe would so quickly forget seemed chimerical. To most Europeans well disposed to the United States, Vietnam was a complex failure of tragic dimensions. They had watched America drift into war, unclear as to the issues or what it wished to achieve, with distorted self-serving emphasis on moral values which it then imposed on the conflict. They shared entirely the judgment of such venerable hawks as Dean Acheson, who by 1967 was convinced that the only option for the United States was to get out, cut its losses—and quickly. Europeans were dismayed by Washington's inability to see the obvious and to disregard the irreparable damage being caused by this hopeless war to American society and to America's position in the world.

To the end, with the exception of de Gaulle, European leaders maintained a discreet silence on Vietnam; there was a recognition that this was America's own crisis. European leaders were sensitive to other ramifications of the Vietnam war. They learned that the Nixon administration was to apply even more stringently than Johnson the use of the Vietnam conflict as the litmus paper to distinguish friend from foe. Canada, Sweden, and Germany were all to feel the lash of White House anger. Official Washington's resentment of ambiguous European support and lack of understanding was matched by the estrangement of the European youth, the socialists, and many of the intellectuals for whom the Vietnam war imprinted a picture of a white, industrial superpower conducting a brutal and brutalizing war against a small, agrarian society, an image which was further to separate Europe from the United States.

The new intimacy between Washington and Moscow became a major source of European anxiety about Atlantic relations. In response to alarms regarding superpower bilateralism carried on over Europe's head, American authorities countered with defensive, even indignant reactions: It should have been evident that the nuclear superpowers, by definition, had special responsibilities; America was only doing what Western Europe had begun at least ten years before and had, furthermore, urged on the United States. On the latter point, Washington ignored the disparity in size which made a qualitative difference—a nuance lost in the confusing dialogue. Europeans felt that America's extensive dealings with the Soviet Union were fundamentally different from those of Belgium, or even France. Nixon's and Kissinger's casual suggestions of some new pentagonal balance-of-power system sent out new waves. The Europeans could see neither the historical analogy nor the contemporary sense in a concept apparently founded on a shifting equilibrium of the U.S.S.R., China, Japan, the United States, and Western Europe. They regarded it as amoral and totally at odds with the premises of the postwar Atlantic alliance, a structure resting on a complex series of interlocking security, political, economic, and cultural components.

The Nixon-Brezhnev intimacy posed a new threat to the Atlantic relationship. By 1973 Europe's satisfaction over the warmth and civility of the Washington-Moscow discourse had switched to concern. Reassurances by Kissinger, for example, that the United States had no intention of exploiting for its own advantage the sharp differences between Russia and China aroused, rather than allayed, suspicion. Europe speculated nervously about the ramifications of the Soviet-American relationship, especially the degree to which it had become the central element in American foreign policy. Just as some Europeans feared that Brandt's *Ostpolitik* made Germany susceptible to Russian blackmail, so Nixon's dependence on his success in Moscow led others to worry about the hold this gave Brezhnev on American policy. The environment became conducive to blossoming rumors on how this new American-Soviet relationship might be used to Western Europe's disadvantage. At the ministerial meeting of the Conference on European Security in Helsinki, Europeans sensed a background of prior, private understanding between Washington and Moscow. These worries and distrust gave the Russians the lever with which to pry at old objectives. Europeans found it hard to believe that the Russians could resist the temptation to play on Europe's apprehensions that its vital interests were topics of discussion, perhaps subject to disposition in the course of private tête-à-têtes. Such suspicions would be difficult to handle in the best of circumstances, but in a sour Atlantic mood they introduced a dangerous complication in European-American relations.

As important as substance was the new American style—unfortunately an abrasive one. To a foreign policy of calculated obscurity, in which secrecy was an indispensable tool, there was added the "Connally method." While the span of the Connally meteor was mercifully brief and the contrasting style of his successor, George Schultz, soothed European sensibilities, the tensions remained and the impact on European-American relations endured. Europeans naturally wondered whether the self-serving chauvinism heralded a new American isolationism. They caught a warning of the appearance of a different America, indifferent or hostile to Europe's political aspirations. They had no desire for some grand deal on which Connally seemed intent, with Europe and America sitting around the table bargaining out trade, financial, and security interests.

The Rome meeting of finance ministers in the fall of 1971 had offered an example of the bite of this method. Secretary Connally, employing the full force of his singular personality, strove to extract from the Europeans both parity realignments and trade concessions. Threatening the Community's finance ministers, Connally attempted to exact from them a commitment by the Community in the trade area. The Europeans tried to explain that, under the constitutional system of the Community, they lacked the authority to give the concession he sought, that, specifically, they were not a "Council of Ministers" acting on an initiative from the European Commission. These explanations were brushed aside as clumsy evasions.

On the American side, Connally aroused latent jingoism and stimulated in Congress and the business community a new and vigorous strain of nationalism. For a country harried by foreign economic problems he offered the easy way out: it was all someone else's fault. Now, at last, Washington would pursue American interest with the same aggressiveness as the foreigner sought his; no longer would negotiations be left in the hands of American officials more concerned with preserving international tranquility than in tough bargaining.

Nixon's embrace of Connally and, by extension, of his ideas and techniques seemed paradoxical. Connally's uncomplicated concentration on the balance of payments and economic advantage to the exclusion of all other national interests was hard to reconcile with the President's contrary absorption with security and political affairs. Seemingly, it was the Nixon moth drawn to the Connally flame—flamboyant, extroverted, self-confident, and Texan. Yet at bottom the two were in substantial agreement. Both were practitioners of adversary relations. Both sensed and were prepared to exploit, admittedly in different ways, the deep American currents running against international cooperation and in the direction of new forms of economic nationalism.

The year 1973 was one of vast change in the attitudes of European governments and their missions in Washington toward the administration. A wariness developed, a conviction that criticism of Nixon's policies were inscribed in a White House black book of foreign enemies. The White House regarded foreign uncertainty and unease as leverage to extract concessions from allies as well as adversaries.

If an Atlantic dialogue had existed, there would have been a means for coping with a worsening situation. But as the Kissinger-Nixon grip on foreign affairs tightened, the normal lines of American-European communication atrophied. The informal, open conversation of the past was replaced by occasional, entirely confidential discussion with foreign leaders by the President or Kissinger, which excluded the State Department and its missions abroad.

The Missing American Bureaucracy

The bureaucracy, especially the State Department, had indeed fallen on evil days. Were it due only to the singular methods of Nixon and Kissinger, the matter could be dismissed as a transitory problem. But distrust, suspicion, and distaste for the Department have always been there to some degree, and the cure must be more than superficial. Despite Kissinger's new incarnation as Secretary of State, Nixon's highly personal system continued, with all that this implied for American-European relations. As an approach to the conduct of international affairs, the technique assumes that the real enemy to be kept in ignorance and at arm's length is the American bureaucracy. At San Clemente during the 1973 meeting with Brezhnev, Nixon relied on the General Secretary's aide instead of an American interpreter. The chance of leaks was less with a Russian official than with a man from the State Department; furthermore, an American official might have felt an obligation to inform the Department of the content of the discussion.

Although there are obvious difficulties and risks of disclosure in bringing a large, unwieldy government into delicate and complex foreign negotiations, there are costs in its exclusion. The knowledge of experts is indispensable to frame and to guide policy. Moreover, by definition, democracy implies openness and involvement and participation of the bureaucracy. This is a part of the essential process of associating American society with foreign affairs; the bureaucracy must be included if the public is to be more than a claque for the President. The similarity of Western European societies demands multiple points of contact across the Atlantic, particularly between the respective governmental establishments. In the dark as to where the United States is or wishes to go, allies are hopelessly perplexed by the shadowy maneuverings at the heads-of-government level. Rather than re-establishing the pluralistic communication when it is so desperately needed, the atmosphere of secrecy compounds the powerful centrifugal forces at work among the Atlantic countries.

We have to recognize, however, that at this stage the government, as a bureaucratic mass, inevitably comes to reflect the nationalistic, quasi-isolationist mood of the country. This governmental orientation results, in part, from the monopolistic control of foreign policy, in part from the reflex behavior of domestically disposed agencies. With hardly more information and understanding than the private citizen, the bureaucracy and its political leaders—the agency heads—regard the Community with thinly veiled mistrust, and conclude that in obscure ways this new Europe works against American interests. Unintentionally the Europeans occasionally give substance to these suspicions. In March 1973, for example, the Council of Ministers rejected a modest Commission proposal to reduce Community tariffs as an anti-inflationary move. In debating the issue, of minimal economic consequence in any event, ministerial comments to the effect that any such unilateral action would give America a windfall sounded like nothing so much as narrow protectionism.

The domestic agencies, only occasionally involved in limited aspects of foreign affairs, rarely see beyond their institutional interests. Burrowing down specialized tunnels, they are immune to suggestions of larger national concerns or of broader foreign policy implications. To the specialist from the Treasury the awkward and ineffective Community institutions are explicable not as deficiencies inherent in a nascent political system, but as a calculated European device to frustrate American purposes.

A vigorous State Department might have filled some of the void created by White House inattention to Western Europe and lack of interest in either the European Community or foreign economic policy. But under Secretary Rogers the once strong Department drifted along on its own odyssey to irrelevance. The problem was to become so serious that many former critics of the Department in the domestic agencies and the Congress began to call for measures to restore its influence. With the departure of Under Secretary Elliot Richardson there was no one at the top level of the State Department attempting to master European policy. The Deputy Under Secretary for Economic Affairs was too low in the hierarchy; the Policy Planning Council had been liquidated, against the unanimous advice of its previous directors; and the European Bureau, reading the handwriting on the wall, discreetly restricted itself to staff and advisory functions.

Whatever its deficiencies, the Department was the sole voice in Washington to argue the case for the Community, to block, where possible, aggressive moves mounted by the domestic agencies against Europe, and to serve as interlocutor for the worried Europeans. At the desk-officer level a handful of officials fought an endless and skillful bureaucratic battle against great odds. Elaboration of policy was impossible in the absence of support from the Secretary or the White House; their achievement was to preserve the broad structure of the past policy.

Already in decline, American embassies drifted even further from reality. The Department of State became a figure of fun, systematically excluded from all sensitive matters, unable even to perform the elementary task of instructing and informing its diplomatic missions abroad. Secretary Rogers could not share with his State Department colleagues the information essential to the Department's effectiveness if he hoped to retain the confidence of the White House.

At a time when the Europeans most needed insight into American thinking, the Department, isolated and ignorant, was in no position to help. In 1972, during a brief period of consultation in Washington, I outlined to Rogers the merits I could see in a meeting between Nixon, the President of the Commission, and the heads-of-government of the nine members of the enlarged Community. With atypical interest and enterprise Rogers asked me to prepare at once a memorandum summarizing the idea, but with the caveat that I deliver it directly to his office rather than by the usual channels. This was the last I was to hear of the matter from any American source. On the other hand, from European contacts I discovered that Rogers and the White House were pursuing the idea in various Community capitals. By this time I had learned enough not to be surprised. When Kissinger and the White House became interested in an issue, American officials would be cut out.

Lack of information only partly explained the growing irrelevance of the diplomatic missions to Europe. Nixon exceeded his predecessors in that distinctive American practice of placing in ambassadorial positions men whose only visible qualification was financial loyalty to the party. The saturation of Western Europe with political appointees made some governments wonder if they were not being cunningly insulted. The

conduct of relations with Europe requires a constant balancing of political, security, and economic factors, further complicated by the degree
to which important matters are handled by international or regional
organizations, especially the European Community. Despite years of
diplomatic experience, most career ambassadors have difficulty gaining
control of this range of subject matter and technique. It is a maze calculated to baffle totally the businessman on his first diplomatic assignment. Almost to a man, the political ambassador's reaction is a retreat
to the clichés of diplomacy, to the routine of bilateral relations, broken
by occasional forays in support of immediate American economic interests as defined by businessmen colleagues.

During the critical, sensitive confrontation and subsequent negotiations
in 1971 regarding parity adjustments and the lifting of the tariff sur-
charge, Washington offered American embassies no guidance or any
indication of its strategy. Indeed, American diplomats were more disadvantaged than the governments to which they were accredited since
the foreign officials, through their Washington embassies, were at least
in touch with their American counterparts in the Treasury during the
course of the protracted negotiations.

During the Rogers regime, in its isolation in Brussels the United States
Mission to the European Communities might as well have been located
on the upper reaches of the Orinoco. It was a world of silence. The
Mission's functioning required more the anthropologist's talents than
the diplomat's. The staff were close observers of the mores of the new
Europeans, gleaning impressions, compiling notes which were duly
transmitted to a headquarters that never responded. Telegrams, telephone inquiries, and personal visits to Washington were fruitless. There
was neither interest nor guidance; there were only murmurs of remote
irritation.

A small risk in this situation was that the Europeans might take seriously the views of the American diplomats in Europe, haplessly believing
that these views reflected the foreign policy of their government. The
desperation of European officials to discover American policy encouraged
them to grasp at such straws. The Mission's way of dealing with this
dilemma was to insist on its ignorance and lack of instructions, while
trying to interpret as accurately as possible what it took to be Washington's attitudes and views. The broad outlines of American policy
could be detected. There were the ritualistic statements regarding Euro-

pean integration. With a degree of crude divination—and hope—the general direction of American policy could be projected. But it was a clumsy process, more witchcraft than diplomacy. Europeans associated with the Community, who should have been closely informed of American political and foreign economic policies, were left in confusion, along with the rest of Europe.

Lost Contacts and Undefined Roles

For those Europeans who wished to restore the Atlantic dialogue and help reverse a deteriorating relationship, the lack of both useful American political connections and information undercut their effectiveness with their compatriots.

By his record, no European seemed more securely anchored to the idea of an Atlantic partnership than Sicco Mansholt. As a Dutch official he was deeply involved in the Marshall Plan and in the integration movement from its inception; he had close American friends; yet his last years with the Commission were marked by a growing anti-Americanism. His metamorphosis in regard to the United States was similar to that of other liberal Europeans. As a socialist he reacted against the oligarchy of big business, American devotion to goods and consumption, Washington's indifference to the misery of poor countries, and an America so long mired in a colonial war which he abhorred. The new breed of American officials intensified the alienation. Had Washington officials sought a closer relationship, the estrangement might at least have been arrested. As possible evidence of this lost opportunity, when Mansholt attacked the excesses of American materialism and urged the alternative Western goals of the quality of life with a de-emphasis on raw economic growth, the texts on which he drew had been sponsored and written by Americans.

The new generation of European youth poses another problem for Atlantic relations. Born yesterday, with neither experience of war nor memory, they are drawn to the East by curiosity, by the attraction of novelty. Stalinism is the shadow of history; reality is détente. What this generation does not know about Eastern Europe it is sure it knows about America. As the European youth see it—with their disdain for American materialism and the Indochina war—the critique had already been written by American youth. Furthermore, the attitudes of many of the most articulate Europeans developed out of their experience as undergraduate or graduate students in American universities, and during the heat of the campus revolts of the late 1960s. Generally skeptical, uncommitted emotionally to the European Community as such, feeling themselves at odds with America, they are part of a generation at best passive regarding European-American relations. It would be hard to discover their foreign policy goals—perhaps some form of unstructured globalism, predisposed to the poor countries; to a degree European-minded, but loosely so. Certainly, they are hostile to the cumbersome bureaucracy in Brussels.

The young, well-trained, and aggressive European businessmen, many of whom have had their apprenticeship in the United States, have their own prejudice against America. There is no hint of deference to the United States, no interest in examining American problems in a larger context, certainly no sense of European obligation to the United States. The mood is cool and competitive, more than ready to defend European positions and policies, and prepared to adopt the adversary relationship if that is what America wants.

Paradoxically, and despite the European wish for greater independence of the United States, Europe still looks to America for leadership. America's attempts, for instance, to induce the enlarged Community to take the lead in the trade field met with Europe's agreement in principle, but with reservation in practice. At this stage of development, international leadership is beyond the Community's grasp. It can react or oppose, but its primitive structure and internal disagreement as to its role and policies preclude effective initiatives.

The Yom Kippur war and the consequent energy crisis exposed with depressing clarity European and American deficiencies. Instinctive reactions were purely nationalistic. The hallmark of American energy policy, improvised in the face of the crisis, was independence. It was not until December 1973, in his speech before the Pilgrims of Great Britain in London, that Kissinger suggested a possible collective approach by the major consuming nations. France and Britain hoarded and hoped to capitalize on their "friendly" status with the Arabs and obstructed efforts led by the Commission and Germany to develop a common European policy and response.

The Middle East war and its aftermath provided a case study of the ills afflicting the Atlantic relationship. The hegemonial power and intimacy of the U.S.S.R. and the United States were dramatically evident, as was Europe's impotence. NATO consultation was forgotten at the height of the crisis, and the Europeans demonstrated that the side-effects of impotence were appeasement of the oil producers and harassing actions against American moves to provide urgently needed supplies to Israel. Kissinger's proposal for an Energy Action Group, in turn, violated a basic diplomatic principle; Washington failed to prepare the ground with the participants, while the Europeans made their sorry contribution by ignoring an initiative which, in different times and under other circumstances, would have been exploited. Europe and America were out of phase.

The chaotic preparations for the 1974 energy conference in Washington dramatized the dismal state of European leadership, the ineffectiveness of the Community, and the inability of the Europeans individually or collectively to take the kinds of international initiatives commensurate with the Community's latent power and own self-interest.

The adverse effects of a passive, reactive Community are substantial. They hinder the capacity of Europe and the United States to find an effective means to explore together major, long-range issues. The specific costs of inaction to both Europe and the United States in the several important substantive fields are bad enough, but there is a further price to be paid. The absence of active collaboration on the larger issues has meant that the interface of American-Community contact has been almost exclusively trade conflict, without the counterbalance of constructive joint endeavors.

As we have seen, there were both Americans and Europeans whose reservations about a united Europe sprang from a conviction that an integrated Europe would inevitably become a third force. The skeptics anticipated that, instead of cooperating with the United States in a true Atlantic partnership, a united Europe would become increasingly independent, with opposition to the United States deemed essential to a separate European identity.

The distinction is subtle between Monnet's and Kennedy's notion of European independence and equality as the basis for a balanced Atlantic relationship on the one hand and, on the other, what has come to be identified as Gaullist insistence that Europe can be Europe and have a personality of its own only by keeping its distance from America. Ironically, Gaullists, or "European nationalists," and non-Gaullists have often agreed on the immediate measures that Europe should take; they have disagreed totally on the objectives of these measures. A strong, united Europe implies a Europe with its own interests, ideas, and policies. Even in those fields where European and American interests coincide, a united Europe will have its own notions of how best to proceed.

In the emerging European-American relationship the problem will be to distinguish between European nationalism in the pejorative sense and the drive for a distinct European identity. If there is to be a united Europe, its leaders must encourage the sense of a new identity. It will always be tempting to establish this personality by juxtaposing the Community and the United States. In order to goad Europe to greater unity, Jean-Jacques Servan-Schreiber, in his book on the technological gap, held up the peril of a Europe absorbed by giant American companies. Another example of European insistence on preserving its identity arose in the early planning for the next major round of trade negotiations. One obvious objective would be the total elimination of industrial duties. The Community rejected this option on the grounds that it would have the effect of dismantling the Common External Tariff. They argued that some protective tariff remained essential to insure the integrity of the Community. In other words, to be a community means to include some and to exclude others. The British were quick to accept this rationale. Despite Commonwealth ties and other world-wide interests, immediately after entry they too argued that certain privileges went with membership: to wit, barriers which create advantage for those inside, disadvantages for those outside. It was part of the process of creating a sense of community and then stimulating a degree of European loyalty to it. Yet the risk is always present that Europe in reaching for identity will grasp only narrow European nationalism.

The quest for individuality can also take the form of a conscious European interest in the search for policies distinct from those of the United States. Some Europeans sought this in Community policies toward the developing nations. Others, especially the French, found it in Europe's special vocation in the Mediterranean region and Africa. They suggested an obligation which derived from historical relationships, but rested on the strategic importance to Europe of the Mediterranean littoral.

While secondary to the sweeping political and economic impact of the Middle East war in 1973 and the energy crisis of 1974, the European struggle for some form of Community response to these situations demonstrated how European unity could breed misunderstanding, mutual suspicion, and bitter recrimination. Depending on the vantage point, Jobert and Kissinger were both defenders of the faith—or infidels. The overt passion with which they flailed at each other during the Washington energy conference and the following month in Bonn and Brussels, as distinct from the close political calculations of each as to the advantages to be gained from the confrontation, by sheer excess obscured rather than illuminated the underlying issues.

Kissinger's sharp reaction revealed the administration's insistence on dominating Western strategy, its demand for uninhibited freedom of tactical maneuver and its propensity for personalizing intra-alliance relations, as well as the low priority America gave to further European unification. Future American administrations would face the same basic problem: Would the United States show tolerance for the slow, clumsy, and probably egocentric efforts of the Europeans to draw together? Nixon and Kissinger had demonstrated the ease with which the most tentative Community policy and limited show of independence could be portrayed as a direct challenge to the American pursuit of a Middle East settlement and to the harmony of the NATO alliance and could even produce threats to review defense commitments to Europe. Washington's manipulation of Europe's first serious attempt to develop Community policy on a crucial issue set a bad precedent. While the dust had settled by the summer of 1974 with the sudden rediscovery of harmony, first at Ottawa and then during the mini-NATO summit in Brussels, the impression was implanted in the American memory that a unifying Europe did not advance but threatened American interests.

Living with Differences

Partnership presupposes mutual, independent thinking and differing analyses and conclusions. It is a relationship which assumes a process of continuing compromise. The contrasting European and American approaches to the international commodity agreements have been one example out of many issues on which there can be quite different but still rational positions. The American view has been that such arrangements are clumsy instruments rarely serving their prime objective, which is to assure stable and somewhat higher than market prices for producers, and that their requirements for intergovernmental control and market organization are at variance with laissez-faire doctrine. The Community, unburdened by this dogma and with a greater proclivity to interference with the market, has looked on commodity agreements as a useful tool to help the developing countries. The Community stands ready to experiment. The history of commodity argeements tends to support American skepticism. Nonetheless, this is the kind of issue which should be susceptible to compromise. By sheer chance, with shortages of foodstuffs and raw materials in prospect, the Europeans' nondogmatic approach seems more relevant and might offer some chance of bringing order to a dramatically altered international market.

In the economic world of the future, each of the major democratic units—the Community, Japan, and the United States—will have to learn to accommodate itself from time to time to the views of others. Thus, the United States must adjust in several ways: recognize that the world is no longer subject to American dominance; consider ideas and approaches different from its own predilections; understand the European desire for independence, and be tolerant if this independence may on certain occasions be employed irresponsibly.

The new European identity can take shape on bases more solid and credible than reflex opposition to the United States. While the similarities in goals, values, and problems of the two continents exist, there are also substantial differences which events of the 1970s have heightened.

In late 1972 Andrew Shonfield, British economist and Director of the Royal Institute for International Affairs, in his third Reith Lecture touched on this point in a general warning on the underlying differences between America and the Community.

"Back in the twenties President Coolidge said, 'The business of the United States is business.' He summed up an important strand in American thinking—which is that governments do best when they simply provide the opportunity for the forces of private commerce to assert themselves. By the same token one might say today: 'The business of the European Community is politics and social welfare.' Again, the Americans, who tend to see this European venture as an exercise in classic New World Federalism, designed to liberate the forces of private enterprise from the interference of national states, are going to be disappointed. For the fact is this is a very interventionist Community, most active in regulating the domestic affairs of its member countries and at the same time annoyingly deficient in clear-cut authority when it comes to conducting its relations with outsiders. From an American point of view this looks like a nasty combination of busy-bodying at home and sloth abroad."[2]

It has become commonplace to remark on the similarities between American and European society since both face what is loosely described as the "American industrial phenomenon," a phenomenon less American than industrial—frozen food plastic-wrapped, urbanization, crime in the streets, pollution, and inflation. One distinction is the matter of time; *when* the problems arrive is more pertinent than *whether* they are American or European in origin. As Shonfield suggests, another difference may be *how* these common problems are attacked. In view of the impact of American or European responses to these problems, substantial variations in approach can create real Atlantic misunderstanding and tension.

Should the United States become wedded to anti-institutional, pragmatic balance-of-power policies, the growth of a not particularly benign form of European nationalism will be stimulated. An Atlantic relationship of adversaries, of deals and close bargains, is incompatible with the system both Americans and Europeans earlier hoped to develop. NATO, the OECD, and the idea of Atlantic partnership all assumed that Europe and the United States were tied together by extensive mutual interests and by devotion to certain common roles which were reinforced by institutions. The earlier approach envisioned a system of cooperation, reason, and law, one benefit of which would be the containment of the excesses of both American and European nationalism—especially as expressed in unilateral action. The Nixon administration's precept that international relations are adversary relations, in addition to calling into question the assumptions on which postwar Atlantic policy have been based, inevitably stimulated adversary inclinations among Europeans. The oppressive imbalance of American and European military power and political influence creates a fertile soil for the very attitudes Washington fears and professes to see. The inherent divisiveness of economic issues had for years been counterbalanced by the Atlantic consensus

2. *The Listener*, November 23, 1972, p. 702.

on defense. By the early 1970s, however, many factors were undermining the earlier reserve strength of this centripetal Atlantic force: détente, *Ostpolitik*, suspicions and disagreements within the alliance generated by arms control negotiations, and quarrels over defense burden-sharing. Pressures in America to reduce military expenditures are matched or exceeded in Europe. Congressional opposition to the maintenance of substantial American forces in Europe coincides with European resignation in the face of this probable development. Thus what has been an Atlantic bond threatens to become a new source of division and disagreement.

The drifting apart of Europe and the United States is evident in another crucial area: the behavior of the bureaucracies. In the murky world of government the conduct of the anonymous civil servant is important. The direction of policy is frequently set by the expert who produces the first draft. The attitude of these career officials regarding Atlantic relations can be vital. If the premise, for example, of the European *fonctionnaire* is to cooperate with America, or if he senses that this is the wish of his political leaders, then the thrust of his work will be in this direction. By 1970 this had become neither the atmosphere nor the practice on either side of the Atlantic.

The extent of change in attitude can be seen in the proceedings of the innumerable, privately sponsored European and Atlantic conferences. Without conscious intent the European meetings have increasingly become oriented toward intra-European questions. Attempts to draw attention to major external problems, such as Japan, are heavy going. Among the young European experts, the organization, the problems, and the policies of the European Community absorb their attention to the exclusion of such tedious subjects as how to cope with a confused and troublesome America.

Over the last twenty years the change in European attitudes toward the United States has been profound. Some of it derives from a strikingly different Europe and its view of itself, some from America's own preoccupations, policies, and actions. America senses all this and its own attitudes are affected by it. The problem is not a matter of determining blame, for much of the change has been beneficial—and more of it has been inevitable—but of understanding it. The danger is that America and Europe will drift even farther apart. Both Europe and the United States have moved from the postwar world of spontaneous cooperation and common purposefulness to egocentricity and indifference to the trans-Atlantic relationship.

An Atlantic "Balance Sheet"

A "balance sheet" of Atlantic accounts can offer a reasonably comprehensive, if rough, approximation of American-European relations. To strike this balance unavoidably involves some mixing of apples and oranges. The inevitable subjective judgements make a balance sheet of this sort vulnerable to the determined critic. Obviously, elements in the accounts resist quantification; for example, the psychological factor was a significant component leading to the international financial crises in February and March of 1973. Nevertheless, it is an exercise which provides a unique basis for evaluating the benefits, burdens, costs, and complaints which are at the center of the American-European debate.

The first major item in the account is the trade balance with the Community. The United States long enjoyed a consistent trade surplus with the Community, running as high as $6 billion. For the first time in 1972, it had a small deficit. But by the end of 1973 the anticipated effects of the dollar devaluations were becoming evident with an American surplus of goods and services of $4.5 billion. Even the rough balance of American-Community exports and imports in 1972, while discouraging to those who yearned for a major surplus with Europe, should have been seen in the context of a global trade deficit of almost $7 billion that year. Thus, in our worst year we did comparatively well with the Community.

In the contentious area of nontariff barriers, taking into account some 800 restrictions catalogued by the GATT secretariat, only Solomon could identify the greater sinner. For what it is worth, the Community interest in negotiating nontariff barriers arises from the Europeans' conviction that the United States has the greater array of such restrictions, and therefore reciprocal reduction or elimination would benefit the Community. Certainly Europe has its battery of nontariff barriers, its agricultural quotas and labyrinthine protective procedures which preclude foreign bidding on government contracts. The United States has its full share of restrictions—from dairy quotas to the disingenuously named "voluntary" steel and textile agreements.

Agriculture, the area of sharpest confrontation, is a debit for the Community and a credit for the United States, although less substantial than conventional American wisdom would have it. As a result of the Common Agricultural Policy (CAP), America lost part of its European farm market. It has frequently faced subsidized and essentially unfair competition in third markets. At the same time American sales to Europe of tobacco and soybean products increased, the latter rising to the incredible figure of $1,713 million in 1973. To a European the United States has been something less than the open agricultural market and the free trader portrayed in Department of Agriculture bulletins. The Europeans have observed a country which has consistently supported income through intricate forms of government intervention, including import restrictions. With respect to the balance, however, had the Community's CAP not existed, American agricultural sales of grains to Europe would have grown beyond the general increases registered until 1973 turned international agricultural trade on its head.

The second major element in the account is assistance to the developing countries. American complaints against the Community in this area include the network of preferential arrangements, especially those with the African and the Mediterranean nations. The charges are potential damage to American trade and sabotage of the most-favored-nation principle and of the multilateral trading system. The Community denies trade damage and points out that American exports to the countries in question have increased more than has the trade of the Community. The Europeans note the generalized preference scheme they installed in 1971, which contributes to the economic growth of the poorer countries. They also recall that while the United States initiated the generalized preference concept, the administration was laggard in approaching the Congress. When legislative approval finally came in December 1974, it was circumscribed in such ways as to make difficult the harmonization of American and European preference programs.

With respect to foreign aid, the United States has a longer history of assistance, larger in the aggregate and more generally distributed, but it now appears intent on rationalizing steadily reduced levels. Community aid is more current, more specific, and, with declining Congressional appropriations, three times the American level on a gross national percentage basis. The Community gains modest credit for this factor in the overall accounts.

Finance is the third major area in the balance. The way in which

America and Europe perceived their complex financial relationships in 1972 and 1973 has some bearing on future Atlantic relations. Contemporary American and European attitudes have been conditioned by events of those years—the August 1971 crisis, Europe's frustrated ambitions to achieve monetary and economic union, the glut of Eurodollars. America feared that the Community's monetary union would work against the international system, that it might turn out to be no more than the nucleus of a European-based financial bloc. Despite the setbacks of 1973 and whatever the long-term implications, there was apprehension that the embryonic European monetary union would disturb an already badly battered world monetary system. America also worried that the distraction to the Europeans of their internal financial problems and the complex objectives of monetary union could encourage further international monetary crises and make the resolution of such crises more difficult. Partly as a reaction to excess Eurodollars and partly due to French importunings, capital controls began to spread. European pressure for dollar convertibility was resented by Washington as unrealistic in view of the massive deficit in the American payments and European unwillingness to facilitate American surpluses. Finally, in the atmosphere of sharp Atlantic competition, Washington feared that American companies active in Europe might be victimized through new Community restrictions on capital movements, discriminatory taxation, and other subtle forms of harassment.

Europe had seen the monetary element of the Atlantic balance quite differently. With no alternative but to live with the flood of some 150 to 200 billion Eurodollars and with no exchange guarantees, they resented the privileged position of the dollar and the fact that the United States escaped the discipline imposed on all other countries. Despite irritation at this inequity and the contribution which excess dollars had made to European inflation, they tampered little with the Eurodollar market. The Europeans emphasized that the Treaty of Rome generously treats American affiliates as national companies, thus contributing to the spectacular growth of American equity investment in Europe—further evidence of an open and liberal Community. They also recalled that they had not attempted to restrict the repatriation of profits and retained earnings.

During 1974, when tolerance and good sense were notably absent, the efforts and the achievements of European and American finance ministers and central bankers were unique. Perhaps because they realized the distinct prospect of financial chaos and had not forgotten the lessons of the 1930s, there was little of the adversary approach which contaminated other fields. Insofar as Europeans thought of Atlantic financial relations in terms of advantage or disadvantage, gainer or loser, they saw themselves as helpless victims. The massive dollar overhang contributed to European inflation; an undervalued dollar tended to distort trade flows; and, despite everything, the dollar remained dominant.

In this economic sector there is no clear plus or minus. While the Europeans appear to have a somewhat stronger case, by varying the weight attached to the several elements, widely different conclusions can be reached. Taking the economic field as a whole, a disinterested observer might conclude that neither side has gained materially at the expense of the other.

The political component of the "Atlantic balance sheet" is more elusive, defying quantitative measurement. Yet reciprocity clearly exists, with patterns of reinforcing political support and, not less important, political understanding and tolerance. The United States has contributed through its early endorsement of European unity and backing for German *Ostpolitik*. Throughout the Cold War and intermittent crises, America joined with Western Europe in meeting explicit challenges to Berlin. The Europeans have welcomed American leadership in NATO and the command of allied forces. Despite adverse public opinion and domestic political costs, the European governments, with the exception of France, largely refrained from criticism of the Vietnam war. With Gaullist France the exception again, Europe supported American disarmament policies and attempts to ease the continuing Middle East crisis. Over the years North America and Europe had developed, to a degree, the habit of consultation on political and security problems. The effectiveness of this mechanism has generally been in inverse ratio to the importance and urgency of the issues.

Disputes over the form of a new Atlantic Charter or whether any such document would serve a useful purpose and disagreement on obligations for consultation (specifically with respect to relations with the Arab states) illustrated what determined men could do to exacerbate relations. Controversy in this area was unexpected. Most students of Atlantic affairs had concluded that the potentiality for American-European conflict lay in the economic field. Regardless of the merits of the noisy arguments over principles of consultation and of European and American performance, it is unarguable that each offended the other, and did so offensively. Therefore, in this sector, too, it would be hard to define one as creditor and the other as debtor.

As for defense, it has become an article of faith in the United States to picture Europe as defended by American soldiers at American expense. During his visit to Washington in early 1973, former Prime Minister Heath complained of this distortion of the situation. He argued that the burden of Western defense is shared on a roughly equitable basis and that what is at stake is as much American security as the defense of Europe. In 1973 the United States had some 2,232,610 men under arms; Europe, 2,764,000. In the NATO area there were about 318,000 American forces; of the European troops, essentially all were in the European theater. Of those based in the Federal Republic, 475,000 were German, 148,000 non-German—the remainder, of course, the American forces. In short, Europe was furnishing 90 percent of NATO ground forces, 80 percent of the naval forces, and 75 percent of the air forces.[3]

The defense slice of gross national product is an accepted measurement of comparability of national efforts.[4] In 1972, American defense expenditures had fallen to 7.5 percent of GNP; for the European Community countries the equivalent figure was 4.3 percent. On the other hand, the Community's GNP is only slightly more than one-half that of the United States. Taking account of the size of the two economies, the imbalance between the United States and the Community is considerably less than appears at first blush. Another measurement is per capita income. The average for the Community countries (which differ considerably among themselves) was $3,180 against $5,056 for America in 1972. The ratio of critical indices—of defense expenditures as a percentage of GNP and of per capita GNP—finds the United States and the average of the Community countries in almost exact equality. These shorthand figures should at least dispel the notion of gross inequity in American and European defense efforts. It is a high price we all pay for propagandistic charge and countercharge, one result of which is an aggrieved America and an indignant Europe.

The balance-of-payments costs of American forces in Europe have

3. Drawn from Institute of Strategic Studies, *The Strategic Balance 1973–1974*.
4. Drawn from SACEUR data, February 13, 1973, "Revised Data on Defense Expenditure and Gross National Product—1973."

been the most nettlesome issue in Atlantic security relations, with reverberations far beyond the defense field. No other subject has produced such a rich array of conflicting statistics. In 1973, the balance-of-payments cost were estimated at $2,242 million, offset by receipts of $912 million. The problem has poisoned the Atlantic atmosphere. As the general American deficit mushroomed and the dollar weakened in international markets, a nagging irritant became a critical issue. It came to mesmerize the Congress, and made nearly impossible an overall view of Western defense or the general setting within which military costs should be considered.

If a distorted view was the American problem, then Europe has been cursed by acute shortsightedness. Since Congress was so inflamed, the failure of Europe to apply imagination to the containment of this issue remains inexplicable. With the new financial regime of floating currencies, the dollar again in demand, and the American balance of payments strong in comparison with that of Europe (Germany excepted), many thought that Congress would finally recognize the issue of defense and the balance of payments as an anachronism. On the contrary. For Congress, nothing had changed. It was as though fixed rates were still applied, as though the dollar were still overvalued and a wealthy Europe were refusing to meet its "legitimate" obligations. One would hope that awareness in the United States of the economic problems confronting Europe, the delicate balance of allied defense, and Germany's contributions to meet the alleged American deficit would keep this problem under control.

The worn generalizations about the basic, long-range values of the American-European relationship are useless in coping with the man who, for instance, by mastering the balance-of-payments cost of American forces in Europe has convinced himself that he has unassailable proof of European freeloading and American gullibility; he proceeds from this case to draw conclusions about the entire relationship. This exercise to put the parts of the large Atlantic picture in perspective runs the risk of encouraging the perverted impression of a static, mechanistic world, of overlooking the intricate interplay of forces, the dynamic nature of American-European relations, and the varying weight given to the various factors at different times and by different people.

From this brief examination should emerge a complex, constantly changing pattern of advantages and disadvantages, with the factors shifting from credit to debit. But the inescapable and reassuring conclusion is the rough balance. Neither Europe nor the United States is gaining significant advantage at the expense of the other. Furthermore, the breadth and extent of interaction in the various sectors should show the danger of concentration on one problem to the exclusion of others, especially in the overall Atlantic balance sheet.

The New Phase: Attention, Recrimination, and Truce

Coincidentally with Nixon's second term, indifference to Europe was replaced by occasionally close and frequently irritated attention. Six months were to elapse after the portentous announcement in November 1972 that the next twelve months were to be the "Year of Europe" before Kissinger, in a speech in New York, elaborated what the United States had in mind. The operative element turned out to be preparation of a new "Atlantic Charter" which would redefine the political, security, and economic elements of the Atlantic relationship. It seemed odd that a former professor of international affairs would elect the most unproductive diplomatic art form, communiqué-drafting, as the vehicle for reviving American-European relations. Under European pressure the proposed Charter would be fractured and re-emerge in more mundane form as a statement of Atlantic principles by the nine and a separate NATO declaration. This exercise dominated the Atlantic dialogue in the last half of 1973, with the press drawing fever charts showing the degree of American content or discontent with the European efforts.

While hardly a bright page in either European or American diplomatic history, the "Year of Europe" was not dull. With no consensus among the Europeans, or between Europe and the United States, the drafting of principles was bound to be contentious and eventually sterile. The nine, slow to react to the American initiative, added to Washington's unhappiness when they reached agreement on a draft in Copenhagen, without American participation. Friction also grew over a trade dispute (the so-called GATT 24:6 issue) where excessive claims of injury by the United States due to the entry of Great Britain and others into the Community produced the inevitable and equally irresponsible denial by the European Commission of any damage whatsoever. The Kissinger-Jobert confrontation during the energy conference of February 1974 was merely a prelude to a series of remarkable American outbursts in March.

Although Jobert was the provocateur, the American onslaught, rather than singling out France as the target of Washington's wrath, was undiscriminating and directed against Europeans in general. Kissinger's sharpest reaction was saved for the efforts of the nine at political cooperation and specifically their proposed economic arrangement with the Arab states.

Europe was almost as startled by the sudden outbreak of peace and harmony in the summer of 1974 as it had been by America's spring offensive. Kissinger's overt pressure and Nixon's threats at Chicago on March 15, repeated in Houston, had dismayed Europeans. While manifestly unable to act positively and collectively, European leaders had the good sense to refrain from responding in kind to the American barrage. Finally, the political changes in Bonn and London brought to power leaders anxious to placate the angry Americans. The greatest contribution to this new mood arose from Giscard's accession as French president and the consequent departure of the provocative Jobert. Open warfare with European allies was hardly compatible with the strategy of an embattled President whose struggle for survival depended heavily on demonstrable mastery of foreign relations. Facilitated by both French and American compromises, agreement was reached on the NATO declaration. Washington rediscovered the merits of formal consultation, with Nixon stopping in Brussels to outline to NATO in general terms the summit meeting he was to have with Brezhnev. Kissinger subsequently gave the post-mortem on the Moscow discussions to the NATO Council, followed by visits to other NATO capitals. While Nixon made no effort to meet with Community officials during his brief stopover in Brussels, Kissinger paid a courtesy call on Ortoli on the edges of his session with the NATO Council. In retrospect it was a policy crazy quilt: four years of indifference to Europe, an announced but undefined "Year of Europe," and a period of fevered but staged controversy were followed by a truce and excessive satisfaction that Atlantic warfare had ceased.

Behind the theater and contradictions of these years there could be detected certain American policy objectives and abiding apprehensions. First, Western Europe and certainly the Community were seen in an adversary role. Nixon stuck a prescient note in his January 31, 1973, press conference. Every reference to Western Europe employed the word "problem." He offered America a dour choice: ". . . what the position of the United States should be and the new, broader European community should be in this period when we can either become competitors in a constructive way or when we can engage in economic confrontation that could lead to bitterness and would hurt us both." The Atlantic relationship envisioned was hedged in by exclusively economic considerations, by problems, and by a tradesman's choice of either constructive competition or confrontation.

Second, what is publicly alleged to be American policy is not necessarily so. American policy toward European unity ranged from detachment and passivity to hostility. The tedious disputes over the declaration of principles and suspicion of attempts by the nine to coordinate their foreign policies exposed an administration by no means keen on Europe's "speaking with one voice." In fact, the faltering efforts of the nine to do so were to be described by Nixon as "ganging up." Many Europeans thought that the Americans sought a role as the "tenth member" of the Community, with Washington officials involved in internal European deliberations from the outset. And again, another facet of American policy was the administration's unwillingness to throw its weight behind those forces in Europe working for greater unity. In the course of several trips to Europe in 1974 and 1975, I was repeatedly asked why, when Europe struggled with its greatest crisis, was there no American support for an embattled Community, as had been the case in the past.

Third, the essence of modified American policy was indifferent acceptance of economic union, attentive of course to injury to American interests, but acute unease in the presence of European political collaboration. The objective was a docile, client-Europe whose proxy would be in the hands of American officials as they went about their negotiations, whether with the Russians or the Arabs. The shock treatment administered in March left Washington with two satisfactory alternatives: a collective but pliant Europe that would follow an American lead, or a fractured Europe where we would necessarily deal with several of the principal European states bilaterally. Ambivalent toward Europe and nostalgic for a bygone world, the Wilson government would be responsive to the suggestion of the "special relationship" in lieu of European-American cooperation. The change in Bonn offered further insurance. Washington calculated that on crucial issues Schmidt, a more nationalistic chancellor than Brandt, would be susceptible to American pressure and if necessary could be persuaded to break with his European partners.

Fourth, for the first time in postwar history an American administration had dealt with Europe precisely as it would a hostile state. Washington's contrived public attacks and overreaction to the Community's labored and substantively limited offer to the Arabs were the tested tactics of confrontation politics. They achieved their objective. Already staggering under the energy crisis, harried European leaders were unprepared to face as well an aggrieved America, apparently ready, for instance, to use the threat of reviewing its NATO defense commitment to win its point. With its basic security at stake, the odds were too high for Europe.

Fifth, the Nixon administration demonstrated no interest in the institutional development of the Community. It neither sought to understand the clumsy, primitive Community system nor attempted to aid its evolution.

Finally, and ironically, Kissinger and Nixon, those eulogizers of de Gaulle and Gaullism, were transformed into francophobes when the clever, irrational obstructionism of the Pompidou government threatened their policies. Kissinger became convinced that European union, especially in the political area which concerned him, would certainly be dominated by the French and thus be anti-American. But once the French election in 1974 was out of the way there was, for the moment, no longer advantage to be gained in attacking the Americans for domestic political purposes. Furthermore, Giscard's style was more supple. As a result, a new amiability surrounded American-French relations, and the apprehension of Europe controlled and manipulated by a hostile France receded.

Despite ambiguity on policy, open dispute, mutual suspicion, and continued purposelessness among the Europeans, this curious period of active Atlantic relations was not entirely bleak. Behind the bombast about consultation, and the lack of it, senior American officials had met quietly with the European political directors. In the end Washington declared a victory in this contest and in effect accepted a Community formula which left pragmatic and informal the mutual obligations to consult. The arrangement was essentially what could have been obtained before the display of pyrotechnics.

There were a few other favorable signs. President Ortoli's visit to Washington in October 1973 had produced signs of a new atmosphere. For the first time, discussions with the President and the Secretary of State dealt with larger matters without the traditional concentration on the tedious list of economic problems. For the Europeans it was a dramatic change. At another level the semiannual American-Commission meetings were becoming routine and admittedly useful. The Commission and the Council of Ministers had awakened from their complacency and recognized the existence of an "American problem." The appointment of Jens Otto Krag to Washington as the Commission's representative was helpful. It was hoped that his credentials as former Danish Prime Minister and former Foreign Minister would provide him with more than adequate political authority to deal with nine touchy member state ambassadors and with the White House and the Cabinet. Indeed, all of the rancor, charges, and countercharges of 1973 and 1974 had at least sensitized Washington to Atlantic relations. It would no longer be possible to ignore Europe or assume sycophantic support of American diplomacy.

Chapter V

Looking to the Future

As with all policy prescriptions, new directions for American policy toward a uniting Europe risk sliding off into academic abstraction of the ideal formulation. Inattention to reality, to the limits which confine foreign relations, combined with congenital American optimism, encouraged the United States to embrace generous but fanciful expectations for the United Nations, to expect instant democracy and economic development through the miracle of "take-off," and, especially, to assume Atlantic harmony based on the natural affinity and common cause of Western Europe and the United States. If foreign policy cast from romantic illusion is one danger, equally gross errors can derive from the mindless extrapolation of the past. The challenge is not to lose all idealism or to discard all past experience, but to blend a judicious mixture of the two with an evaluation of change and an identification of trends. Change, in fact, so dominated the early 1970s that it threatened to obliterate all other factors.

Some basic trends, common to both Europe and the United States, seem strong and irreversible. These include American preoccupation, governmental and private, with domestic matters and a declining commitment to foreign affairs. Specific documentation of the "new isolationism" was the contribution of a study commissioned by the Potomac Associates.[1] Scientific polling and careful analysis led to the conclusion that by 1974 "the completely internationalist percentage had dropped to almost one-third of what it was ten years earlier, from 30% to 11%." Lloyd Free, who designed the survey, concludes that while this adverse

1. Donald Lesh, ed., *A Nation Observed: Perspectives on America's World Role* (Washington, D. C.: A Potomac Associates Book, 1974).

trend does not signify a return to pre-World II isolationism, ". . . it does signify that there has been a remarkable break in the internation-alist consensus in the United States. At a minimum, the 1974 results indicate that the stalwart internationalism of the earlier years has been significantly eroded." The decline in internationalism stems from the loss of traditional optimism, the waning sense of America's omnipotence, and a lessening of interest in maintaining America's predominance. The basic change in attitude can be seen in the answers to this proposition: "We shouldn't think so much in international terms but concentrate more on our own national problems and building up our strength and prosperity here at home." From 1964 to 1974 those who agreed with this conclusion rose from 55 percent to 77 percent.[2] Slight imagination is required to see the impact of this shift in opinion on Atlantic relations.

By the early 1970s an atmosphere of unreality surrounded American foreign policy. Nixon, whether in times of strength or weakness, gave this field absolute presidential priority. Whatever may be the later judg-ment of historians, it is noteworthy that the public praised his foreign policy record uncritically, even as his popular support evaporated and impeachment loomed. The American public apparently associated for-eign relations with spectator sports, games to be observed, but with no personal involvement. And the manner in which the President and his Secretary of State played this game, excluding rather than involving the public, weakened the earlier consensus in support of American foreign policy. The Nixon-Kissinger formula placed few onerous demands on the general public, such as demanding sacrifice in the form of sharing limited oil resources with hard-pressed allies or increased export of food to meet the desperate needs of famine-threatened areas. There was also the question of whether the popular image of the administration's diplomatic achievement could survive the revelation of its clay feet through possible collapse of the the South Vietnamese government, a détente which evidently served Soviet purposes while damaging Western interests, stalemate or worse in the Middle East.

A tragic irony could be the result. A President whose fascination with foreign affairs was complete may, through his diplomatic style, have handed on to his successors a quasi-isolationist nation. With the American constituency for international involvement diminishing, with

2. Ibid., p. 144.

confidence in government seriously eroded, a domestically oriented, cynical America could severely limit the freedom of maneuver of future executives. An assertive Congress, indignant over the Johnson-Nixon war in South Asia and bent on redressing the balance between the legislature and the executive, could compound the problem. Instead of cooperation between the equal but separate branches, so indispensable in the American political system, and innovative foreign policy, the more likely prospect could be enervating confrontation between the two branches, resulting in a paralyzing stand-off, or reluctance on the part of future Presidents to become involved in "unprofitable" foreign relations.

Attitudes toward the European Community

It is improbable that the public's hazy image of the European Community as a hopelessly complicated affair will change substantially in the near future. Its attitude toward Western Europe has reached an equilibrium at a low level of casual interest. However, the coincidence of Community enlargement and international economic crisis has replaced this complacency with a new, obscure worry that European developments contain some unspecified dangers to American interests. The acrimony and cross-purpose during the Yom Kippur war and Washington's manifest displeasure with European behavior did nothing to quiet the public's unease. Unable to see the pattern in the tangled skein of Europe's activities, the average American is content to limit his view to his own immediate interests or to a familiar and narrow functional outlook on finance, trade, investment, national politics, or defense. The dangers of distortion in this restrictive approach are ignored, and little effort is made to see Europe whole.

Each American group has its own special set of concerns. To the American farmer the European Community conjures up little more than the Common Agricultural Policy. His gloom seems partly a matter of cultural lag, for it gives small weight to the consistently strong European market for soya products and tobacco and the dramatic shift in 1973 to a seller's market for agricultural products. The professional supporters of liberal trade doubt that the Community will be liberal; they foresee European protectionism as an inevitable outgrowth of an inward-looking Europe. They find confirmation of their expectations in the Community's preferential arrangements. American industry and the multinational companies fret about their prospects. Will the Community's industrial and social policies introduce discriminations against foreign firms? Few business observers optimistically project the positive experience of the past into the future. The American economist has a crabbed view of the future Community. Brushing aside political goals, accomplishments, and hurdles, he sees little but confusion and problems. In a profession which places a premium on cynicism he is ready to demolish each proposition: the Community, he insists, is unnecessary, for the economic benefits would have occurred in any event; inevitably the Community will become more egocentric and inward-oriented; the Europeans lack the institutions and the will which would enable them to solve the intimidating problems surrounding economic and financial union, to say nothing of the energy crisis. There is an almost masochistic satisfaction in the expectation of victory for the forces of inertia—for the Community's dissolving into a collection of national states, seeking contentment through conspicuous consumption, foregoing European union for a customs union with pretensions. These are generalizations, of course, with many exceptions, but they represent the prevailing, skeptical trend among various groups of Americans.

After years of indifference the Congress has become uneasily aware of the vast change in process in Europe. In January 1972 the House Ways and Means Committee went to Brussels, the Committee's first trip abroad. Close on its heels a delegation from the House Foreign Affairs Committee appeared in Europe to explore with the Community continuing exchanges with members of the European Parliament. The prospect is for more, although still limited and essentially spasmodic, Congressional attention. Unfortunately, the interest, stimulated by specific problems, will continue to lack focus, perspective, and continuity.

The few Americans actively engaged in European affairs feel the absence of general interest or support. The liberals and the youth, groups that tend to coalesce on certain issues, see Atlantic relations in negative terms: "How can policies conceived two decades ago possibly be valid today?" Their principal strands of thought, which intertwine, are revisionist history and preoccupation with détente. Aside from the handful associated with the self-perpetuating Atlantic Council and the Atlantic Treaty Association, the general public attitude toward NATO is passive support but with growing concern over defense expenditures in general and, specifically, the balance-of-payments and budget costs of stationing troops in Europe.

Even the American "European" enthusiasts are on the defensive, challenged to explain how great tasks can be accomplished by a Europe riven by disagreement on policy and organization. Were they wrong in anticipating that Europe would, through unity, have the strength and momentum necessary for a renaissance of its international responsibility? Does not the recrudescence of nationalism doom the great dream of community and condemn the new Europe to little more than a consortium of national states?

Analysis of these attitudes and trends offers little encouragement. In the absence of renewed efforts by both sides, relations between the Community and the United States, although clothed in the rhetoric of the past, promise to be distant and cool, with an undercurrent of antagonism which can turn mere disagreements into outright conflict. Doubts and suspicion with the flavor of animosity could come to rule opinion. The lack of any clear policy leaves American opinion fluid and uncertain. Unconsciously, the country appreciates that the old Atlantic policies and relationships no longer adequately meet the requirements of the present-day world. There is a sense of drift, no sense of urgency, no concern that the Atlantic world may be moving out of control, no hint of advantage to be gained from this formative period in European affairs.

The Critical Period Ahead

Throughout the turbulent postwar years, America provided a firm foundation, the stable element in an unstable world. American leadership, ideas, and self-confidence brought order and progress and preserved the peace. Acclaim for this role was not universal; some resented America's casual arrogance, the occasional insensitivity, and imprudent action. It took the recent signs of American uncertainty and withdrawal to remind Europeans how much the international order depended on an assured United States, openly pursuing known policies. Predictable policy and behavior came to be seen as more important than whether Europe agreed with all elements of the strategy and tactics—or even whether Europe entirely liked the America it had to live with.

Neither American policy nor behavior is any longer predictable. While many past lines of policy have been either discarded or emptied of meaning, little has been offered to fill the vacuum. Slogans and maneuvers are not substitutes for clear policy and comprehensible strategy.

The weakening of American resolve and the loss of direction arrived at a bad time. Few of the old problems had been solved, but each day added new ones to the agenda. Economic development turned out to be an objective, a hope rather than a program; the roles between heretofore eager raw-material sellers and reluctant industrial buyers were suddenly reversed; man's casual destruction of his physical environment was called into question by the interest in its preservation; population control moved from cultural taboo to the status of a recognized but almost insoluble practical problem; in place of the primary sanctity of international contract, the summary abrogation of agreements was becoming routine. A purposeful and involved America might have rallied latent Western ideas and forces.

As contrasted with the stark and unambiguous threats of the past, the future East-West relationship appeared obscure and not without elusive danger. That "détente" has no exact meaning was symbolic. The flexibility of the Soviet Union seemed more tactical than strategic, more a response to economic necessity and to the challenge of China. The new phase of East-West relations made more urgent the solution of problems, for instance, those flowing from the complicated relationship of mixed or market economies with the state trading systems of the East. Whether the Soviet Union's moderation is means or end, temporary or permanent, the crucial point is that its policy to a considerable extent will be formed in response to the world it faces to the West. If the Atlantic democracies fall into disorder or recession or into economic conflict with one another and compete in a race toward unilateral disarmament, then Soviet opportunism will be encouraged and Moscow tempted to pervert détente into a means of exploiting Western disarray.

The irony of détente has been the transposition of European and American positions. In the early 1960s the Europeans took the lead to ease tensions with the East, despite American reserve and caution. In the 1970s it was Nixon who made the shift in policy a visible reality. Then, as America belatedly rushed forward, several Western European governments, made cautious by experience and aware of the limited freedom of maneuver available to Eastern Europe, had second thoughts as détente brought not a weakening but a tightening of the Soviet Union's economic grip over Eastern Europe. While arms control negotiations were pursued at the international level, qualitative and quantitative improvements were made in the Soviet defense system; simultaneously with the Conference on Security and Cooperation in Europe, the Soviet government intensified internal pressure against political dissidents and intellectual freedom; Soviet political and military power were accompanied by deep economic difficulties.

One fate the Europeans fear is "Finlandization." George Kennan dissected the term and found it empty. He argued the inapplicability of the notion by finding Finland's situation "unique." He went on to suggest that its neutralism and international economic arrangements were ". . . in large part voluntary—a matter of policy on Finland's part—and they have not been unduly onerous."[3] Next, Kennan suggested that worries about some similar evolution in Western Europe derived from the unwarranted suspicions of possible changes in American policy and doubts about the stability of the American commitment. He alleged that European fears arose from the military imbalance (nuclear and conventional) between the U.S.S.R. and Western Europe, a disparity traceable directly to Europe's deficiencies, particularly to flagging political will. (One cannot argue with the latter part of this proposition.) Kennan dismissed the assumed dangers of an asymmetrical military balance and concluded that either the Soviets would not utilize their superiority, even for political purposes, or, if they should attempt to do so, Western Europe could ignore the pressure.

In point of fact, for Europeans the term suggests an unplanned, thoughtless slide, through the confluence of many events, into a situation not dissimilar to that of Finland: a degree of neutralism, limits on economic freedom as a function of European fragmentation, with each state accordingly more vulnerable to external pressure. Europeans agree with Kennan's impatient judgment that, with the Community's imposing size and industrial strength, there is small excuse for the East-West political and military imbalance which nourishes Western European apprehensions. In their view, Finlandization could be Western Europe's future if it fails to react to a series of predictable, dangerous phenomena —Eastern military forces strengthened under cover of détente, expanding East-West economic relations while Western defenses erode, an

3. *Foreign Policy*, No. 14 (Spring 1974).

abrupt and substantial reduction of American forces in Europe leading to recrimination and fading confidence. Kennan scorned the Europeans for their doubts about the American commitment to NATO; yet the Potomac Associates study noted, "By 1974 only 48%—less than a majority—felt the United States should honor its NATO commitments by coming to the defense of its major European allies."[4] Is European unease entirely irresponsible?

In effect, Kennan argued that Finlandization will not and need not come about if only the Europeans will be sensible and organize their affairs rationally. On this all can agree. The term is invoked precisely because of their anxieties about the future: a disputatious and adversary atmosphere aggravated by common absorption with internal issues and, consequently, weakened ties between Europe and America; domestic pressures and demands in successful competition with defense expenditures; the mounting crisis of European economies and, thus, of capitalism; and, without examination of actual performance, rejuvenated interest in Marxist alternatives. Rather than meet these real or fancied events with renewed efforts toward greater unity and cooperation in defense programs, Europeans are haunted by the prospect of retreat into more intense nationalism, with each nation concentrating its efforts to hold what it has. In this situation the Soviet Union could bring its military strength and the cohesion of the Eastern bloc to bear on individual and wavering Western nations. The interference in Western internal affairs could begin discreetly—pressure on various political parties to support certain Soviet foreign policy positions; endorsement of, or opposition to, present or potential Western political candidates sufficient to make or break them; pressure against further steps toward European political unity and influence employed to frustrate Atlantic policies. To those who cry "fantasy," the Europeans point to the object lesson of Russian interference in Finland's internal affairs, of the attempts to intrude Soviet views into Austria's domestic political life. Rampant nationalism, combined with a possible breakdown of the Western defense system, gives a certain plausibility to this model of European disintegration.

Arms control and disarmament negotiations have the potential to produce further disorder in Western ranks. With the ambivalence in-

4. Lesh, cited, p. 144.

herent in democratic societies, the allied nations are pulled in many
directions by conflicting interests when they attempt to determine arms
control policies. They find it excruciatingly difficult, as an alliance, to
agree upon common positions. To complicate matters, the future stages
in arms limitation cut directly across Western European defense interests
to a degree not true of SALT I. It is conceivable that American troop
reduction and further movement in arms control would force the Europeans to pull together, but in the view of recent European history (for
example, their response to the monetary crises) this would seem but
a pious hope.

The rich nation–poor nation relationship is replete with new difficulties. If the United States is the Western pace-setter, more by default
than by desire, then its performance during the early 1970s with respect
to the developing countries is a dismal omen for the Atlantic future.
The first reaction of the European nations was neither to follow the
American lead and reduce their aid efforts nor to cut back their generalized preference program. But European society is subject to the same
kinds of domestic pressures that are at work in the United States. European interest groups, for instance, gathered inspiration and argumenta-
tion from the success of the American textile industries in forcing
restrictions on imports into the United States.

The trade and payments system established after World War II was
made for the familiar world of nation-states. Almost casually the Western countries supervised the construction of the new system. The emergence of the new nations, however, dramatically altered this situation.
The GATT began with 23 nations but, by 1973, had an unwieldly
membership of 83. The national self-consciousness of these new states,
most of which were on the lower rungs of economic growth, revitalized
the old notion of juridical equality. Therefore, the organization of
international economic affairs was complicated by a host of new nations
with interests and problems different from those of the old, industrialized
countries and by the rejuvenation of nationalism.

The fact that the international economic system can neither be
preserved nor improved in the absence of collaboration among the Community, the United States, and Japan poses traumatic problems for the
smaller advanced nations. The interests of these countries, such as
Canada, Sweden, Australia, Mexico, might be protected by the international system and its supporting institutions, but the weaknesses and

disrepair of this system offer these countries little to lean on. Furthermore, the worries, problems, and proferred advice of the smaller countries have little impact on the economic superpowers. A possible reaction will be for these nations to turn inward and embrace a new nationalism, as has Canada.

One could not deduce from the puzzling evidence where American foreign policy was leading; it was easier to guess what the policy would not be. The Nixon-Kissinger era has left to future administrations a heritage of priorities, prejudices and style which limits their maneuverability. It would be difficult, for example, to restore confidence in international institutions or interest in the elaboration and enforcement of multilaterally agreed rules. The Nixon administration's approach to the OECD was indicative of its attitude toward Atlantic organizations. In 1973, with economic relations moving from argumentative to critical, the OECD was a logical forum for concentrated consultation. Yet, for a year and a half the administration ignored the necessity of naming a successor to the American ambassador to the OECD when he was transferred in November 1972. To insure that no one would miss our lack of seriousness, Nixon then appointed to this specialized job an obscure business protégé of Senator Goldwater. Rather than continuity and predictability, a pattern of instability and surprise had been set. It would also be difficult to break the habit of separating words from acts; the one-time Attorney General John Mitchell had won immortality with his aphorism, "Don't pay attention to what we say. Watch what we do."

The pursuit of immediate self-interest had become the touchstone of American foreign policy. During Nixon's first term, even without the burdens of Watergate and uncontrolled inflation, the administration showed little disposition to engage the prestige and power of the White House to divert or check domestic economic pressures inimical to constructive foreign relations. With Presidential authority in question, both the will and the capacity to stand up to the interest groups melted. Ironically, while Nixon fought for expanded, nondiscriminatory trade relations with the Soviet Union, few efforts were mounted to counter the many actions which worked against allied or neutral interests. In fact, the handling of the financial crises, the shortages of meat, soybeans and feed grains, and, finally, the Arab fuel embargo suggest quite the contrary.

Ten years after the Trade Expansion Act of 1962, new legislation was clearly indispensable, as was a further round of international negotiations. The course of the enabling legislation through the Congress and the unusual cross-currents in the trade field reveal little of the future. All one could say with certainty was that old patterns of behavior were not being followed.

The defection of the AFL/CIO from the ranks of liberal trade was complete. While the substantive bases for this turn-around were hard to accept, the emotional and propagandistic rationale was not. With unemployment high, the massive investment abroad by multinational enterprises coincided with a dramatic increase in imports. The AFL/CIO laid this change in the trade balance to the goods produced abroad with cheap labor by the "runaway" corporations. Thus the residual protectionism of labor could be enriched by its classical aversion to big business. Furthermore, AFL/CIO election support in 1972 put a sizable number of congressmen and senators in the debt of the unions.

The administration's proposed legislation went off on a new tack. In addition to the normal request for tariff-cutting authority, the White House sought to placate enemies by seeking the right to impose restrictions and to retaliate. The House Ways and Means Committee, under the strong leadership of acting chairman Al Ullman, first developed a bill distinctly superior to that submitted by the administration and then put it through the House with a large majority. The legislation bogged down in the Senate over the essentially extraneous issue of most-favored-nation treatment for the U.S.S.R. This seemed the only aspect of trade policy to catch the interest of the President or the Secretary of State. As the life of the 93rd Congress ran out, the handling of the bill by the Senate Finance Committee showed the changing mood of the Congress. Penalties were written in against the oil producers (OPEC); the legislation was to be both carrot and stick to dissuade raw-material producers from adopting similar cartel practices. It was a nationalistic piece of legislation with a clear bias against the GATT and multilateral procedures. The Trade Act of 1974 was a new knife—all blade, it could be used to cut duties, or to cut imports.

With respect to trade policy, 1974 and early 1975 were significant for what did *not* happen. Against all the odds, trade legislation, of a sort, was enacted. Those congressmen and senators obligated to the AFL/CIO failed to make their expected repayments in the currency of protectionist measures. Congress did not try to deal with the worst economic crisis since the 1930s with the traditional rain dance of new barriers against imports. The Europeans, facing similar problems and pressures, also resisted demands for restrictions either against member states of the Community or outside countries.

It was a picture of negative achievement. But the future remained obscure. The American administration demonstrated no enthusiasm for leadership; a full turnover in the office of the Special Trade Representative hardly signaled a sense of urgency and serious negotiation. There was not the slightest sign that the Community might be ready to fill this void. The Europeans were evidently content to join with the United States in going through the motions of negotiation, assuming that any serious effort would come only after the 1976 American elections.

The enlarged Community will be evolving an identity and arriving at internal agreements on several basic policies less by design and orderly procedure than by accident and force of events. European and American attitudes and policies toward one another will be more affected by caprice than by the thoughtful plans of governments and negotiation. Europe's excuse is that the Community is still gestating, has yet to reach the point where it can make coherent policy or develop in an orderly way its new relationship with America, as Europe's disorderly efforts to come to grips with Kissinger's appeal for a new Atlantic Charter demonstrated. In the heat of argument, with all perspective discarded, it became commonplace in the early 1970s to ignore the degree to which the changes in American-European relations were a function of progress (the development of the European economy) and a reward of success (the growth and expansion of the European Community).

The fates seemed determined to test the Atlantic nations. As America was drawn inward by its internal problems and economic crisis and by declining interest in an unmanageable world, Europe, although spared the searing experience of Vietnam, was caught in its own economic maelstrom and its new nationalism, unable to answer the basic question: what kind of Europe? The almost intuitive postwar consciousness of common Atlantic problems and interests lost its strength as nations struggled for survival, as the deteriorating climate encouraged suspicion and mutual readiness to do battle. The Atlantic nations had no chart by which to navigate; they were without the self-corrective safety devices of the past.

During the war and postwar years, more kindly fates gave to Europe and the United States leaders with a long view, the will, and political strength to sacrifice where necessary the immediate for the larger good. Leadership generated public support. The special camaraderie of the wartime experience of men such as Eden, Macmillan, Schuman, Bevin, Acheson, Lovett, Dulles, Adenauer, Hallstein and McCloy eased crises and left open avenues through which solutions could be explored. Instead of this intimacy and mutual trust, the relationship had become brittle, directed by men to whom that earlier period was already history.

American-European relations raise all the most sensitive and complex problems of contemporary life—the dominance of economic factors, general issues and unifying patterns lost in the mass of technical detail, the blurring of defense, economics, and politics into one another. The harried, average man has neither time nor inclination to become an expert. He looks to his political leaders to master the subjects, to give him a sense of what the problem is all about, and to reassure him that the matter is being attacked intelligently.

One psychological reaction to dismay in the face of highly complex problems is to intensify the search for the simple solution. The Atlantic situation has all the components which lead to this response: involved substantive and institutional problems overlaid with a time factor. The demand is for a device, a committee, a new Atlantic Charter—in short, the quick cure.

Conservatism, on the model of Edmund Burke, offers another answer. As it judges man more evil than good, more incurable than curable, a passive pessimism seems the sensible response. When detached, conservative skepticism is applied to the Atlantic relationship, it can be argued that a grand design, a strategy for blending together the variegated interests of Europe and the United States, is wildly utopian. The conservative-realist might conclude that the rational policy is minimalist, with its active element a matter of perpetual patching-up. The appeal of this approach is undeniable, for it is tailored to the talents of modest leaders.

A conservative-minimalist policy can also dignify and legitimatize the adversary relationship. Once one assumes that man's natural state is competitive and that the life of nations is Darwinian, with the strong weeding out the weak, international relations become manageable, a matter of simple automaticity. It begins with a precise appreciation of one's own interests, which are then pursued with zeal. Appreciation of the problems and interests of others is irrelevant; the basic assumption is that one's adversaries employ the same approach and will take care of themselves. Foreign relations of this genre are uninhibited, except for avoiding moves which would hinder rather than facilitate the achievement of immediate objectives. Predictably, a nation subjected to this adversary policy will be driven to reply in kind.

The adversary relationship is singularly congenial to a country as large and powerful as the United States, whose economic life and interests remain largely domestic and where egocentric, nationalist policy still has strong appeal. The technique holds out attraction to the pragmatist with its de-emphasis on obligation to international rules. It requires little or no differentiation between allies and those who, in a simpler world, were called enemies. The adversary role fits neatly Soviet-American relations, for it is a derivation of the Soviet method, its indifference to cooperation and institutions and its concentration on national interests within what is assumed to be a hostile world. It is a technique natural to any political system which consolidates power in a few hands. It seems especially congenial to generals and to lawyers. But does it suit our relations with Europe?

The cumbersome yet open machinery of the Community, with its diffusion of authority, makes the more polished versions of the adversary technique impractical. But the technique's egocentric overtones, its pragmatism, and the fact that it places such emphasis on reactive responses are bound to attract the Europeans. Indeed, even without the American example, the Community's natural inclinations encourage a certain adversary overtone to its relations with the United States. There is, therefore, a ready alternative to a thoughtful, planned, and responsibly administered Atlantic relationship. If this should be our future it will develop haphazardly, not as the result of conscious choice. Once established, however, it would be endowed with the status of policy, thanks to the genius of rationalization.

If, as Servan-Schreiber suggested, abrasive, self-serving American policies or actions were to be the new catalyst of European integration, no one's interest would be served. This course would impose on Europe substantive positions only coincidentally related to its own real interests; the primary motivation would be the election of policies different from those of America; it would deify conflict rather than cooperation which is basic to European internal stability, growth, and security. Fortunately, it is not a *modus vivendi* that comes naturally to Europe although it did to de Gaulle. Only gross American errors could drive Europe to this option.

The Special Character of European-American Relations

While relations between Europe and the United States cannot be isolated from their interaction with other policies and other areas, nonetheless they cannot be subsumed under other policies. One of Washington's consistent errors has been the attempt to force relations with the Community into one of two familiar patterns: either to treat a unifying Europe as though it were a traditional nation-state, or to regard the Community as merely another international organization. The attraction of each approach was that it drew on established patterns of thought and behavior. For years several American administrations had tried to obtain for the European Community mission in Washington the traditional diplomatic privileges and immunities. The matter stuck on the fact that the mission obviously represented neither a nation-state nor an international organization (the test of the latter was whether the United States was a member). It was finally resolved in 1972 when Congress enacted special legislation to take care of this oddity.

Responsible American policy toward Europe must take into account Atlantic interdependence. Each major functional area—trade, finance, politics, defense—has its own inner bond of interdependence. In addition, there is the interrelationship among these fields, between economic relations and security, between policies toward the less developed countries and the supply of raw materials. Experience has shown that attempts by either the United States or Europe to develop and sustain substantially different policies will fail. As several countries floated their currencies, others were forced to follow. Protectionism in America has fueled protectionism in Europe. Reduced defense efforts by the Dutch or the Norwegians strengthen the hands of those in Congress who would reduce the American commitment to NATO. The irony of the unilateral nationalistic action is that it succeeds only if others fail to react or to adopt the same measures.

In the contemporary world shock waves travel fast. In response to pressure and to meet a political obligation, President Kennedy initiated the practice by which Japan "voluntarily" reduced cotton textile imports to the United States. Rather than an isolated program, it was the precursor of a worldwide movement, drawing in more countries and more products. After ten years, the reverberations of the "short-term cotton textile agreement" continue. Other textile-importing countries insist on similar restraints. "Long-term" has replaced "short-term." In January 1974 a new multi-fiber international agreement came into effect covering wool and man-made fibers. Pressure groups insist that the same restrictive technique be applied to other products. Consequently, other nations can draw on these precedents to seek relief from the United States by "voluntary" American restraints when exports threaten to disrupt their markets.

By 1974 oil had become the witches' brew of the West. Its magical properties metamorphosed Europe and America, magnifying and distorting the latent weaknesses of each—nationalism, regionalism, selfishness, the inadequacies of multilateral and national institutions, the failures to foresee problems and to plan in the face of unmistakable dangers. Europe's collective achievement was to be political appeasement. Despite a challenge to the Community of unprecedented dimensions, the heads-of-government of the nine failed at their December 1973 meeting to agree on the normal summit platitudes or on the elementary first step of data collection. Confronted by a massive problem the components of which were energy shortages, financial chaos, virulent inflation, and recession, the Community members embarked on one more effort to employ the old unilateral techniques. American leadership was late and ambiguous. Far less dependent on imported fuel than Europe or Japan, Washington's quick and revealing reaction to the crisis was Nixon's announcement of "Project Independence," or American autarky. On a separate track, Kissinger's belated efforts to develop a common approach were tentative and confused, with the suggestion in December to convene a group of "senior and prestigious individuals" superseded in early 1974 by Nixon's invitation to heads-of-government for a gathering of high officials in Washington.

As interdependence increases so does the need for more extensive, stronger international rules and institutions to insure that these rules are observed. For twenty-five postwar years, when the United States held a position of economic pre-eminence, by and large it employed its power responsibly, more interested in creating an orderly international system than in using power to dominate. Now, with Western Europe's and Japan's rise to positions of comparable economic strength, some Americans are tardily drawn to the notion of brandishing power the United States no longer monopolizes in the illusion that the exercise of such power would be accepted by docile partners without retaliation.

Since the Community for a considerable period of time will be a reactive body, it will take its lead from the actions of the world about it, especially from the United States. Reluctantly, always slowly, it will respond to liberal American policies; it will, on the other hand, react more easily and quickly to restrictive, nationalistic American moves. The decisions of the Community, still more an assembly of national states than an entity, are hard-fought compromises. Perversely, the rule of unanimity, contrary to so many Community interests, sets limits to Europe's capacity to retaliate. The Commission or an aggrieved state, urging retaliation, can be stymied by the objections of even one member country. Although the rule of unanimity brakes and may moderate Community action, this procedure is not likely to prevent indefinitely a decision by the Council of Ministers if the provocation is sufficient and persistent.

One aspect of the Community's relations with Japan illustrates this point. In the late 1960s the European Commission, with German support, urged that the Community negotiate a general arrangement with Japan which would supersede the restrictive agreements France and Benelux had been able to impose on Japan in the late 1950s. France and Benelux, however, resisted relinquishment of their unilateral rights to impose quotas or other restrictions, and their positions hardened as Japanese consumer electronic goods began to penetrate the European market. The first phase was Community paralysis, to be overtaken by the member states' consensus away from the initial, cautiously liberal Commission proposal, and finally a restrictive consensus close to that of the original French position. In this situation the Community was reacting to two phenomena: first, the strength of protectionist sentiment among the French, Dutch, and Belgians and their ability to obstruct; and, second, the sober lessons Europeans had drawn from American behavior in the face of Japanese imports. The Germans were being driven toward the position of their more fearful and protectionist partners.

If interdependence is a fact of life, logic demands a strategy of conscious and systematic collaboration by the United States, the Community, and Japan. Their collaboration would not have the betterment of the three as its exclusive objective but would be the means to extend and strengthen the international system. Unfortunately, this is neither the strategy about to be adopted nor the direction in which world events are moving. The United States pays lip service to the international system, its rules and institutions; the Community displays somewhat greater, but still passive, interest, while certain of its actions have done much to drain the content from the articles of GATT. As late-comers to GATT, the Japanese were able to gain membership only by accepting discrimination. For years their multilateral and bilateral diplomatic activity with respect to trade matters was diligent, but insignificant in comparison with Japanese devotion to mercantilism. Only in 1973 did Japan see the limits and dangers of the latter policy. It was a good omen that the major GATT round of trade negotiations was inaugurated in Tokyo in September 1973 and coincided with the Japanese shift in priorities. Despite the reversal of Japanese policy, under the surface strong forces in Europe and the United States were ready to urge Atlantic collusion against Japan.

The crises that the Community has met and overcome, its momentum, the commitment of European political leaders, the energy of new members, and a sense of manifest destiny argue that there will be some form of European unity. But as far ahead as one can see, it will be an imperfect union, full of inconsistencies, frustrating to those inside and outside. While one hopes the central institutions, such as the Commission, will play a more significant role and attain greater authority, the balance of power will remain with the nine member governments vis-à-vis the Community. America must recognize that contradictions and conflict are inevitable aspects of the process, not signs of collapse. In this disorder, the dissenting minority in Europe must be kept in perspective. It covers a wide spectrum of political life: a majority of the Labour Party and most British unions, Britain's own xenophobe, Enoch Powell, a few ultra-Gaullists, and some but not all of Western Europe's Communist parties. The disparity and political anachronism of this opposition unintentionally strengthen the case for the Community. Europe's acceptance of a vague goal may also be politically adroit, more helpful to the cause than specific commitment to precise, and probably unrealistic, programs and timetables.

Recent events have shown again the problems of growing up. The summit meeting in October 1972 and the enlargement of the Community had generated a new optimism. In the early months of 1973 the work of the new Community had gone well. But in August 1973 Jacques Chirac, then French Minister of Agriculture, presumably with government encouragement, launched a sharp attack on Germany, charging Bonn with offenses ranging from neutralist tendencies to sabotage of the CAP. Coincidentally, a spate of new stories, attributed to British civil servants, alleged that Community membership had been an economic disaster for Britain. After two decades of crises and prophecies of imminent collapse, however, Europeans tended to discount these alarums, to regard them as inevitable aspects of the Community's evolution.

Relations with this Europe will be difficult. It would be convenient if the Commission were the Community "government" as is the executive branch for the United States. Yet in only the most limited areas, for instance with respect to competition, does the Commission have clearcut executive authority. The energy crisis illustrated the limits of Community competence and the weakness of the Commission. With respect to political matters, during the Gaullist era the Commission was invited to participate with officials from the member states only where its constitutional responsibilities were specific. America must appreciate, however, that this is not a static situation. The trend, osmosis perhaps, will be in the direction of greater Commission responsibility. In part, this is due to the end of Gaullism and the advent of the new pragmatists, but also to the fact that a number of critical problems confronting the Europeans cannot be managed by the Council of Ministers or by *ad hoc* arrangements among nine governments.

Washington is left with the problem of how to work with this Europe. There can be no exclusive channel. The force of habit of bilateral relations and the inertia of large national bureaucracies mean that Washington is almost bound to err in the direction of attempts to do its business with the member states. There is no "correct" working relationship between the United States and the Community; but if Washington, as a matter of policy, determines that it wishes to work with the Community, then American bilateral relations with the member states will tend to support this objective and fall into place.

Forced to deal with the Community, Kissinger clearly would prefer to work with the Council of Ministers rather than the Commission. The attractions of this course are obvious. The Council is the locus of power; furthermore, this means dealing with foreign ministers. Consistent with this prediction, Kissinger met with the nine ministers in December 1973. But they made it clear that it was not a Council of Ministers. No member of the Commission was present, nor, for that matter, was the American Ambassador to the Community. The net result was minimal, if any, substantive progress; nothing was done to enhance the role of the Commission or to impress upon the Europeans the confidence of the Secretary of State in the President's representative to the Community.

Neither the United States nor any other third country can do business directly with the Council. The U.S. Mission to the Community, for instance, does not make representations to the Council, to its president, or to the secretariat, as it does to the Commission. Attempts by Washington to bring direct pressure to bear on the Council have been ineffective or damaging, resented by the ministers as intervention in their internal affairs. An analogy would be a foreign government making a démarche directly to the House or the Senate while those bodies were debating in advance of voting on specific legislation. It would be improper procedure; more important, it would fail. But foreign views can be effectively presented to the Congress by way of the responsible committees or through contact with individual congressmen. Similarly, it is possible and desirable to influence the Council members indirectly through the capitals or through the permanent delegations in Brussels well in advance of the Council meetings.

The Case for an Active American Policy

A crucial question is whether American policy toward the Community should be active or passive. The adversary relationship or the detached, spectator role are variations of the passive approach. An active policy does not imply attempts to impose American views, or to share with Europeans responsibility for the design and development of their Community. It requires, however, a close, sophisticated, sympathetic, and continuing assessment of Europe's own interests in unification, the trends in attitudes, and, particularly, the choices before the Europeans with respect to next steps. The premise of an active policy is a deep

American interest in European unification as a matter of profound importance to the United States.

One major basis for an active policy seems almost hackneyed: the strategic significance of Western Europe—its geographic location, economic power, its vital importance to Western defense, and the priority which the Soviet Union gives the area. A truncated Europe composed of independent nation-states reduces the significance of several of these factors; without unity, advantages and power translate into disadvantages and weaknesses. In addition, the European goal of economic and political unification has special relevance to the complex problems of the Western world. If the Europeans succeed in devising a means to preserve the national and cultural differences of the participating states while constructing a new, common political-economic entity, with real but limited authority, they will have made a profound contribution to contemporary political thought.

Unless America's European policy is posited on a conviction of the importance to the United States of European unity, the dead weight of the Washington bureaucracy cannot be moved from its instinctive hostility or the country from an inchoate aversion to the Community as a current nuisance and as a possible future menace. It is instructive and discouraging to consider the contrast with American policy toward China and Russia which has been marked by careful preparation, patient execution, and the subordination of lesser or diversionary issues. For good strategic and tactical reasons the Nixon administration brought about the reversal of policy toward China and pushed for new agreements with the Soviets. To succeed in such fundamental change required Presidential conviction and determination. Private and governmental forces in this country hostile to the new course were cajoled, pressured, and outflanked as the administration persisted in its purpose. Washington concluded that our national interest would be served by strengthening the hands of those in Peking and Moscow who wished to move in more constructive directions, both in terms of internal and international policies.

We have eschewed neutrality or passivity in our active diplomacy toward the major Communist nations. American policy toward European unity, however, approaches neutrality. Indeed, many Europeans complain that it has been a neutrality tainted with aid and comfort to the minority in Europe opposed to unification. The European legatees of de Gaulle's opposition to the Community have not spent sleepless nights worrying about a policy of active support for a united Europe emanating from Washington. Was there mockery in Washington's approach which put the emphasis on cooperation with Russia and China while its vision of relations with Western Europe and the enlarged Community was one of rivalry and abrasive competition? We have transposed friends and enemies.

It has become a diplomatic cliché that interference in the internal affairs of others is counterproductive. As a diplomatic axiom, this is too simplistic. All too frequently this diplomatic "principle" is brought into play to rationalize American inaction, or as a weapon to employ in the course of internal bureaucratic struggles. The cousin of nonintervention is passivity, which can mean many things: that one is incapable of arriving at any decision, or that one is indifferent to what happens, or that the issues are assumed to be inconsequential, or that neutrality, consciously or unconsciously, will in indirect ways influence the decision-making process of the other side.

America has a real stake in the policies the Community adopts. The policies range from matters which are primarily internal and frequently highly charged politically—for example, road transport, social and regional policies—to those, such as Community policy toward Eastern Europe or the associated countries, where the international implications are clear. In a few areas, surface transport for one, European policies of great importance to the members of the Community are of no consequence to the United States. American interests, however, can be deeply affected by what seem to be purely internal Community programs. The social policy will contain extensive provisions covering the conditions of employment and protection of workers, which will touch equally European and American enterprise. The Community's regional policy could have an indirect impact on American trade and investment.

The motivation behind these policies is to improve the quality of Community life. America should have two basic concerns with respect to such policies: that they should be consistent with our support for a strong Atlantic partner, and that American interests will not be accidentally or unnecessarily harmed. Obviously, worker participation in the management of companies promises to affect European and American industry alike. But if the impact is even-handed, there can be no basis for official American intervention. Presumably, an American subsidiary resident in the Community will find ways within the bounds of good sense to comment on the merits of the various proposals, as European concerns do, during the long gestation period before such policies are finally adopted.

Policies that threaten to discriminate against American interests or to damage the working of the international system should be subject to discussion, as should similar American policies. The European CAP and American agricultural programs are classic examples of policies, ostensibly developed to meet internal economic and social disiderata, where the impact on international trade is real and direct.

To the extent that there is an answer to this problem, it must be found in closer, pliant American-Community relations. If American officials follow sympathetically and seek to understand European objectives and the problems they face, it should be possible, within limits, to avoid nasty surprises or European actions which could harm American interests unintentionally. But there must be full reciprocity. Both branches of the United States government will have to expect, even to welcome, European comment on American policies which seem entirely of domestic moment. This intimate relationship is merely part of the definitions of interdependence.

The idea of active policy stirs the ghosts of such heavy-handed American interference in European affairs as Dulles' offensive in support of the European Defense Treaty just before its death in the French Assembly and allegations of excessive zeal by subsequent American administrations in support of the Multilateral Nuclear Force. If Dulles' efforts in behalf of the EDC had succeeded, his diplomacy would have been applauded. This raises a nice distinction between the conviction with which a policy is held and the manner in which it is carried out. Some observers, looking back, conclude that the miscarriage of both the EDC and the MLF is a tacit argument against conviction and active diplomacy. Rather, it may just as well suggest a need to re-examine the execution of policy, the soundness of the tactical plan, the quality of training, and, especially, the guidance of the individuals involved.

Inner doubts about European integration were reinforced by the problems the movement confronted and the predispositions of Kissinger and Nixon. It was routine for a new administration to assert that whatever had been done before it would do better; or that what should not have been done would cease. As an example of the former, the new administration would sort out American relations with France; as for the latter, America would no longer immerse itself in internal European affairs. This preference could be brought under the mantle of the "Nixon Doctrine" of low profile and reduced American commitments—a policy which had the virtue of codifying the disengagement already underway.

The European Parliament offers an example of an area in which an active American policy could be to the mutual advantage of the Community and the United States. The further development of the Parliament is a difficult problem in theory and also a sensitive political issue, one in which America has a vested interest. An elected Parliament with some minimal power over money and legislation is obviously essential to a democratic Community. But beyond this fundamental truth, there are other American interests in the further development of the institution. Even in its present feeble state the European Parliament, organized not on national but on party lines, is a counterweight to the Council of Ministers, which has a penchant for secrecy and narrow, national bargaining. The Parliament has been the persistent if unsuccessful proponent of a strong, independent Commission. It has shown more active interest in American-Community relations than either the Commission or the Council of Ministers. And finally, the Parliament, even in its present form, reflects the broad, if shapeless, popular European support for unity.

This uniquely European problem is not unrelated to the more general dilemma faced by all parliamentary democracies. Whether the House of Commons, the French Assembly, or the House of Representatives— or the European Parliament—each confronts similar, baffling issues. Legislators, overwhelmed by the complexity of modern life and government, forced to give ground before aggressive executives, find themselves at the same time the lightning rods for mounting public anger against government. A general search is on to find the new role of the elected representative and to restore his place in government.

In this context the political and theoretical challenge facing the Europeans is bound to interest those congressmen and senators directly involved in the reform of the United States Congress. They are in a position to make an expert's contribution to this European problem. Such an exchange need in no way be a trespass into European affairs; rather it could resemble the lively sharing of ideas among the American colonists, the British, and the French in the late eighteenth century. Normal diplomatic channels are a poor means to express American interest in a political problem of this sort. Furthermore, a disinterested, almost academic relationship among parliamentarians would produce valuable collateral advantages in addition to whatever substantive assistance the American legislators might offer. A larger, constructive role for the Congress in international affairs is clearly desirable. At a time when American diplomacy has become excessively personalized and normal links have been weakened by European and American deficiencies, the Community and the United States both stand to gain from supplementary institutional connections.

Many avenues exist. Europeans, especially members of the Parliament, as well as German and British officials, became alarmed about the carelessness, if not irregularity, with which the accounts of the Community were kept. As a result of a visit in mid-1974 to Brussels, organized by the Atlantic Visitors Association, the Comptroller General of the United States, Elmer Staats, was brought into contact with Community authorities concerned with this problem. The Europeans were impressed that the General Accounting Office had evolved into an innovative institution, responsible to Congress, not to the executive, with functions running far beyond the traditional audit. Mr. Staats' discussions laid the groundwork for future informal assistance to Community officials, including an invitation to Europeans to visit the GAO in Washington as observers or as interns. Personal contacts between Europeans and Americans, resting on professional interest in common problems, can be a significant bond in the Atlantic relationship. An active policy toward Europe implies attention to such opportunities.

Current Handicaps: Errors, Omissions, and Mismanagement

If the United States is to have a successful policy toward the Community there must be Presidential commitment. Without it the government will not move, the Congress will obstruct, and the public will remain bewildered and apathetic.

When it feels strong, Europe is likely to throw its weight about; when weak, it can be even more irritating in irresponsible actions, demands, or no action at all—a tiresome partner. To some extent the latter is in compensation for its still imperfect union and military (nuclear) dependence on the United States. If the political conditions and motivation are understood and America concentrates on cultivating a constructive relationship, this can reduce debilitating European resentment. Only a concerned and involved President can assure that the various elements of the trans-Atlantic relationship are kept in proper perspective.

A necessary chore—one largely ignored by Washington—is to provide the American public with a flow of information which puts Community policies and actions in context. Obviously the Europeans have a major responsibility for informing Americans, but their efforts have been modest and without any general plan of how to get at the complex problem of American ignorance and torpor when it comes to European affairs. There is also an American obligation. Although Washington cannot sweep problems under the rug or ignore harmful European policies, evident governmental appreciation of the political and economic crosscurrents that produce European actions would inhibit the needless inflation of contentious issues. American criticism, free of any hint of understanding, has been unrelenting with respect to the Common Agricultural Policy and the Community's preferential arrangements. Until Kissinger's Pilgrims' speech at the end of 1973 there had been no instance in recent years when a senior Washington official had spoken extensively of European union; no one had attempted to explain the political and economic reasons which led to these policies. A sense of proportion would develop if Americans were helped to appreciate the degree to which such policies reflect the hard process of Community compromise, the need to appease domestic European political forces, and the extent to which Community decisions are as much a matter of accident as of design.

The United States, with peculiar insensitivity to Western Europe, misplaced elementary diplomatic tact. It is difficult to imagine how Washington could have expected anything from Europe other than unease over the sudden intimacy between America and the Soviet Union. The contrast was too blatant between the attention given Soviet gymnasts or Chinese acrobats and the routine and impatient treatment of European visitors. More than its incivility, Washington demonstrated its lack of interest in the Community, withholding that subtle but important support which attention implies.

American callousness toward Western Europe owes something to de Gaulle's brutal diplomacy. His grand and spectacular rudeness sank into the American consciousness and became an inarticulated excuse for riding roughshod over European sensibilities. The General defied the rules of Atlantic decency. Many Americans would happily seize this precedent in Atlantic affairs to dispense with normal international courtesy.

If American blindness to the political forces at work within Europe is a problem, then the question is how to get at it. A handful of academics find European unity an absorbing subject, and their conclusions are cautiously hopeful. These are the spectators. They can hardly be expected to turn and reshape public opinion. The players, officials with power to act, see the Community unencumbered by subtle considerations of European political objectives or the problems of transition. The usual Washington attitude is thinly veiled impatience. Ignorance and unconcern about the internal economic and political problems of Europe offer obvious comforts; they free one's mind to concentrate on one's own interests.

Washington refused, for example, to acknowledge in 1971 and 1972 the narrow margin for maneuver available to Brandt with respect to agriculture. The French were on one flank with their absolute priority, the continuance of the CAP. On the other side were the Free Democrats (FDP) whose participation in the government was essential to the survival of Brandt's coalition. Ertl, FDP leader and Minister of Agriculture, was the indispensable man. The problem was politics at its most elementary level. Despite Brandt's obvious dilemma, Washington nonetheless repeatedly demanded that the Community price levels be drastically reduced and that more efficiently produced American farm products be accepted. After years of unsuccessful attack on the CAP itself, Washington disingenuously shifted its position and said it accepted the principle of the Community's farm policy, objecting only to its price levels and controls. These demands had no effect on the farm policy, but they hardened French determination to give nothing—and embarrassed Brandt. It was hard to believe that, had it been within his political power, Brandt, as Chancellor and leader of the SPD, with inflation a major problem and industrial workers the core of his constituency, would not have been delighted to see lower agricultural prices and cheaper food.

American political naiveté has been evident in stereotyping France as incurably Gaullist. The persistence of objectionable French policies which originated during de Gaulle's regime is sufficient proof to many Americans that Gaullism is endemic. This stereotype ignored the suspicious caution of Pompidou and his internal political problems. He had to judge the threshold of pain the ultra-Gaullists would accept without openly revolting. To disregard this internal French political scene displayed more than American ignorance. It allowed Washington officials their facile preconception that the Community would not merely be dominated by France, but by Gaullist policies as well. The simplistic nature of this analysis put the small band of Community supporters in the United States on the defensive, as it frustrated the Europeans who foresaw a quite different Community and wondered at their partner's superficial perception.

Political ineptitude characterized Washington's attempts to insert itself into the 1972 negotiations when the European neutrals were working out their association agreements with the Community. American overreaction and distortions of prospective damage did not influence the course of the negotiations, but did succeed in harming America's standing with Europeans generally. Since the economic life of Austria, Switzerland, and Sweden depends on the close ties with the enlarged Community, America's vociferous criticisms amounted to a rejection of their most basic national interests. In an economic sense the neutrals were already an integral part of the Community, without membership or the rights of members; having as much as 80 percent of their trade with the Community, they had no choice but to reach an accommodation. It was evident, too, that the existing Community members and the four applicant states would insist on an agreement with the neutrals. The determination by the Community to conclude association agreements arose as much from a sense of moral obligation to the European democracies as from economic interests. America ignored these economic and political motivations despite its own broad interest in the material well-being of the neutrals, in their political stability, and their close association with the enlarged Community. Washington's recognition of these simple truths would have significantly improved the atmosphere and might even have engendered in some Europeans the desire to consider open-mindedly the complaints of the United States. Because of the excesses of the American reaction, neither the Community nor the neutrals were moved to dispassionate examination of American claims of injury.

The Nixon administration had no one at the senior level who looked at the Community whole and in the largest setting. In the years preceding British entry, relations with the Community degenerated into an undifferentiated advocacy of any and all American complaints against Europe. There were no responsible officials with authority to suppress trivial complaints and to guide the government along lines which promised to advance substantial American interests. The test of sensible policy is the likelihood that the actions proposed have some chance of success, do not contain unacceptable costs, and take political implications into account.

Some Washington officials, aware of the complexities of the European scene, had an inkling of what America's priorities should be. But they became victims of a policy of appeasement: the nationalistic, protectionist American forces in this country had to be placated. In other words, they rationalized that responsible and liberal foreign economic policy is possible only if the objections or objectives of dissenting groups —Congress, agriculture, labor, business or textile—are satisfied. Many demands of the interested groups rest on wholly specious assumptions, are unreasonable and, if satisfied, can lead to lasting damage. The appeaser's response to the canard that American negotiators have always been outmaneuvered is not to prove the contention false, but to acquiesce and promise in the future that negotiations will be in the hands of tough businessmen, led into battle by the Treasury.

When in trouble, domestic groups cast about first for a foreign scapegoat. The path of appeasement is seductive. If Congress has convinced itself that European border taxes violate GATT rules and discriminate against American goods (despite the fact that both contentions are wrong), the reaction of the appeaser is to accept the charge, to join in the alarm on the theory that he will gain credibility, friends, and a credit to be drawn on later. Missing is Pogo's honesty: "We have met the enemy and he is us." It would be an error of equal dimension to ignore all complaints or refuse to make the compromises which are basic to the democratic system. There must be enforcement of the laws and expeditious handling of anti-dumping and tariff escape clause actions which coincidentally respond to the strong views of Congress. The danger lies in appeasement for its own sake. The satisfaction of each dubious case creates a precedent for equally specious cases. This process does not play itself out in isolation. The Community watches, has the same kinds of internal pressures, and can easily be led to adopt the same tactics.

All countries have a latent desire to export domestic problems. Unfortunately it is an export which induces imitation. The ambiguity of American complaints and their occasionally unconscious frivolity (as in a protest to the Community against regulations which might have restricted the sale of American cut flowers to Europe) in time breed resentment. Extravagant arguments or assertions of excessive damage merely stimulate counterargument, for the temptation to snipe at the flimsy case is irresistible. By 1972 this process was well advanced with Americans and Europeans exchanging exaggerations. The sterility of the debate has been less important than the effect on both American and European public opinion. The public usually ignores the substance or the significance of the case, but feels the heat of the charge and countercharge. What is left is a sense of being wronged. After years of such conflict it is hardly surprising that America's residual impression of the Community is of European restrictions and harm to American interests. As this impression hardens, another obstacle to sensible Atlantic accommodation is created.

There is an urgent need today not for complaints to be shouted over an economic wall but for a responsible, continuing dialogue between America and Europe. This will occur only if the United States government sets the tone by emphasizing the larger, constructive, mutually advantageous aspects of American-Community relations. With such a framework the inevitable problems fall into perspective. To insure that differences do not become the totality of the Atlantic relationship, problems should be handed back to quiet diplomacy. During the cross-Atlantic confrontation which followed the August 1971 currency crisis, Connally's initial list of demands included unspecified European concessions in the defense field. As the battle intensified. Kissinger strove to get the issue out of the hands of the Treasury. Defense Secretary Laird, rather than issue public threats, then took the matter up privately with the defense ministers. He extracted concessions from the Europeans without the scars which the Connally treatment left.

As an example of undramatic diplomacy, Clarence Palmby, then

Assistant Secretary of Agriculture, worked out with Commission officials a small package which involved a trade-off between the Community and the United States of lard and chicken subsidies. In the end, agreement escaped the two parties. The Department of Agriculture feared that somehow the Community, which had not been in the market, would subsidize exports to Latin America. Overreacting, the United States also pressed for a greater reduction of Community subsidies than Commission officials believed possible. On lard, each side agreed to cut its subsidies equally. The Community ingeniously selected a base period when the figures were so high that the proposed mutual reduction had no practical meaning. Before this disagreement could be negotiated, the supply-and-demand situation had so changed that the problem lost its urgency. Thus the history of these first attempts is less than glorious. It was, however, a significant effort at a new approach. Palmby and Louis Rabot, the Commission's director general in charge of agriculture, were serious; the weak point was the absence of support at the political level in Washington and in Brussels.

The lesson in both instances was that a professional, nondramatic approach can work and can encourage as well a cooperative atmosphere conducive to progress in other areas and on other problems.

Chapter VI

The Specifics of a New Policy: Economics

Despite the dazzle of politics, economics remains the basic element in the European quest for unity, and a major factor in America's view of the world. For centuries, diplomacy was a political game, with the economic element there, to be sure, but hidden. Today, relations between Western Europe and the United States derive substantially from the sum of the economic contacts, problems, and, especially, from the wisdom which goes into the management of these relations.

The many issues and the intensity of the disagreements have obscured America's basic economic interest in Western Europe. With the Community's economy moving toward the post-industrial stage, demand should remain strong for the advanced technological products that rank foremost among American exports, depending, of course, on the capacity of the United States to maintain its competitive position. Despite the wild gyrations of international agriculture in 1973 and 1974, the Community should continue to be the richest and most significant commercial market for American farm products although it seems inevitable that it will fall short of our farmers' limitless expectations. American private investment in Western Europe, already of critical importance, should grow and, with the exponential rise of return on these assets, make an ever larger contribution to the United States' balance of payments.

American Investment and European Industrial Policy

With foreign equity investment the most dynamic element in American international accounts, we have a fundamental interest in insuring that the favorable Community climate toward investment continues. This poses once again the question of priorities. A prime American objective should be to avoid exacerbating relations with the Community, especially in the form of uncontrolled trade disputes. It is a risky delusion to assume that trade, finance, and Community industrial policy can be dealt with as though each exists in a hermetically sealed compartment. Americans have misled themselves in believing that the hot pursuit of trade issues and a general belligerence toward Europe will have no collateral effects on other United States' interests. It would not take much to provoke the Community into devoting its considerable, obstructive talents to the harassment and restriction of American investment—and to justify this as a part of the Community's industrial policy.

One of the strong forces behind European union is the desire for equality with the United States in the research, development, and production of sophisticated equipment. This is one reason for the Community's obsession with industrial policy. In approaching the subject, the Europeans weigh a variety of measures. Some of these are essentially neutral and aim at the elimination of artificial barriers among themselves: agreement on a common Community patent policy, a European Company Statute, and the harmonization of laws to facilitate European mergers. At the other end of the spectrum are programs which would imply direct Community intervention, if not supervision, including subsidies and preferential governmental procurement. Precipitated by the Colonna Report of 1970 and after extensive debate within the Community, general agreement was reached regarding the need to dismantle the various barriers and to encourage the creation of Europewide enterprises. This is the familiar process of grubbing out the forest of accumulated national encumbrances which today hinder the development and operation of larger European units. The disagreement within the Community is less over the attack on these hindrances than on whether there should be *dirigist* policies in support of the broad objectives, for example, some form of continuing Community intervention in the business decision-making process, or general governmental support with money and contracts. Just below the surface lies the question: Should the growth of European business be at the expense of existing foreign investment?

Even with respect to the relatively uncontentious, neutral measures, agreement within the Community is difficult to achieve. The enlargement of the Community further complicates matters. For example, the British bring to the Community both impressive technological and industrial achievements (like computers and aircraft) and, at the same time, major problems (like shipbuilding). The inherent complexity of industrial policy, national differences, and difficult judgments as to the efficacy of alternative economic remedies have effectively precluded any comprehensive Community program. It would be risky, however, to assume that inaction will be the permanent response to this challenge.

In its approach to this question America must take into account several critical factors. First is the depth of European interest; second, the variety of policies and instruments available and being considered, and the substantial difference of opinion within the Community; third, the inevitable Community concentration on just those industrial areas where the United States is dominant—aircraft, nuclear technology, computers, and space technology; fourth, the direct and indirect, conscious or unconscious, influence of the United States on the decisions which will be taken.

Apart from its intrinsic importance, industrial policy raises most of the sensitive and difficult questions of attitude and approach that America must consider in its general relations with the Community. Since European conditions have been so favorable to American business, quite naturally the first inclination of American management is to resist all change. But something must give. General obstruction of European ambitions by the United States would generate pressures which would in time produce an explosion. Rather, wise American policy will take into account the Europeans' motivations, policy objectives and interests, and the variety of instruments available to them in achievement of their industrial goals.

In view of the ponderous pace of the Community, there will be ample time for American business and Washington to think the matter through. America will be tempted to exploit the cross-currents in Europe and to cheer on the opposing forces in order to perpetuate the *status quo*. Any such general spoiling action would work against the long-range interests of American firms. Their investments are in Europe because American management anticipates a strong, expanding European market and sees itself not as an economic opportunist turning a quick trick, but as an established part of the European scene. As such, American business cannot disregard the reasonable desires of the Europeans, for as permanent guests in the Community the Americans must share those desires. If the Community can make progress on certain aspects of industrial policy, for instance in removing tax barriers to mergers and enacting the Company Statute, some of the pressure will be reduced; and the Community will be less likely to impose direct restrictions on foreign investment or adopt extravagant or discriminatory stimuli to aid indigenous firms. Those businessmen who believe they see the Community as the future European menace might reflect on the economic adventurism of the Labour militants, such as Wedgwood Benn, who combine an appetite for nationalization with bitter opposition to European integration, and who, among other things, see the Community as capitalism incarnate and a fearsome hindrance to socialist experimentation in England.

As the European debate unfolds, American influence, governmental as well as private, should favor the more neutral, nonrestrictive options. This is an example of an active policy. It is a valid approach, however, only if one assumes reasonably good sense in selecting the issues to be supported and the manner in which this is done. The development of European standards provides an example. There must and will be common Community standards. The decisions reached will have profound effects on American products. Attempts to block this European effort would be injudicious and, what is more to the point, would be inevitably unsuccessful. In fact, there has been quiet cooperation among the Europeans, the American government, and business. Through its contacts with the Commission, the U.S. Mission in Brussels provides the information on the work going forward within the Community which enables American business to get in touch, at the outset, with the Commission's expert working groups. An American contribution at this early stage is helpful rather than intrusive; the assumption is that the Europeans are engaged in developing Community policy, not in finding ways to harm American interests. Timing is crucial. Successful persuasion or intervention is in inverse ratio to the finality of the proposal. If the American governmental or private approach comes late in the Community decision-making cycle, internal European views will have hardened to the point where modification is unlikely, and even the most sensible suggestion can be attacked as shameless intervention in Community affairs.

Most of the component parts of the Community's nascent industrial policy are not discriminatory; indeed, they are similar to statutes or programs already in place in the United States: antitrust, public works, and public supply procurement. In such areas as food and drug legislation and restrictive business practices, low-key exchanges between American experts and Community officials can be useful in guiding the United States and the Community along compatible policy lines and in generating an atmosphere of cooperation. The tough case is obviously much easier to handle in a congenial Atlantic climate.

European industrial policy will be influenced by the fear, suspicion, resentment, and general ignorance which surround the multinational company. It should not be overlooked that these companies are usually American. The notoriety of ITT's Chilean caper has rubbed off on other, entirely innocent American companies. The case has been seized upon by those Europeans who have been pressing for a European Communications Company (which would be made up of the existing national telephone, postal, and telegraph entities) as another argument in support of this ambitious venture. For a continent where socialism and anti-capitalism are articles of intellectual faith, the doings of Harold Geneen, Dita Beard, and others, not to speak of ITT Director, John McCone, with his CIA experience to draw on, confirm the image of the rapacious corporation which the European intellectual learned to recognize at his mother's Marxist knee.

The multinational company has the potential to become either a new source of Atlantic conflict or, with effort, a common problem to be addressed unemotionally and rationally. Because there are numerous, large European corporations whose activities raise the same unanswered questions of public policy as those of American companies, the elements for a joint European-American approach are present. The objective would be to enlarge on the similarity of interests. How do the international corporations operate? Do they escape local taxation through intra-company transfer? Are they a significant source of the speculative pressures on the monetary system? Can the companies be brought under effective governmental control without destroying their unique flexibility and efficiency? Should international rules be devised, and, if so, how should they be administered? If the problems are not approached in this manner by both government and business, the multinational company can degenerate into one more object of trans-Atlantic controversy.

Economic and Financial Union

Even in the expansive, economically peaceful climate of 1972 and 1973, monetary union was an audacious enterprise, dependent for success on collateral economic actions and the political determination of the member states. Europe was found wanting on both scores, well before British renegotiation and the financial crisis of 1973–74 swamped all grand ideas and drove the Community back again to mere survival.

While ill-fated, the Community's initial quest for economic and financial union had one bright footnote: it did not become an area of Atlantic conflict. During that interval, when it was advanced as the next major block in the European construction, any hint of American reservation or opposition could have severely damaged American-European relations. Generally sympathetic, American authorities did not criticize the scheme so much as they doubted its feasibility. This questioning attitude was similar to the worries of many European experts. American restraint was the more impressive since the Treasury had never been notorious for its support of European unity; moreover, it was a tantalizing target for those with critical instincts. The ingrained skepticism of the professional economist turned to cynicism when he compared this financial Shangri-La with the record of procrastination and failure in the Community's attempts to tackle the simplest, most evident tasks of financial harmonization.

The spreading web of trade and general economic interests and commitments among the nine will force the Community, at some juncture, to resume the unfinished business of financial unity. Rather than return to the 1972 blueprints, a new approach is likely, perhaps growing out of the inescapable need to manage the financial and balance-of-payments implications of the energy crisis. It is less important, and certainly less rewarding, to guess at the new approach than to accept and support the conclusion that there can be no effective Community without monetary union. For America to pursue such a policy will not be easy.

The sheer magnitude and urgency of the West's financial plight push to one side long-range and presumably peripheral goals, as the faltering reform of the IMF demonstrates. As treasuries and central banks struggle to survive the storm, instinctive responses are traditional—the use of existing bilateral and international instruments. Furthermore, Germany's aversion to a role as European banker and the Labour government's determination to go under, alone, but flying the British flag, encourage nationalistic tendencies throughout the Community. In light of these considerations and the technical complexity and worldwide scope of the problem, anyone urging that some attention be given to the relationship of immediate financial actions to European monetary union will have a hard time. But while the ideas and the lead must come from Europeans, America should be poised to react in favor of such initiatives.

It is to our interest as well as to theirs that Europe speak with one voice. The United States cannot bring it about, but there should be no grounds for European doubt that America fully endorses the goal. Another way Washington can help the process is in the economic and financial policy activities of the OECD. Chiefly because of the European member governments' unwillingness to give up their national prerogatives, the OECD is still a conglomerate of independent countries, with the nine Community members wearing their OECD hats and acting as national representatives. This traditional intergovernmental atmosphere will not change unless the Europeans take the lead. But at the same time the United States is not without ability to exert influence if it wishes to do so. American officials from the Council of Economic Advisers, the Treasury, the Federal Reserve, and the State Department have the opportunity to point out the anachronism of the situation: How can the nine European states, which act as a unit in trade, with broad political and economic ambitions, participate individually in the OECD as though the European Community did not exist?

The Major Issue: The Trading System

Ironically, trade has come to be the centerpiece of Community-American relations. Investment, industrial policy, shoring up and improving the payments system all fade before the controversies over trade, regardless of their intrinsic importance. Is the future relationship to be determined by the sugar content of canned fruit, by subsidies on lard, chicken breasts and legs? It matters not that the trade-tariff issue becomes of less and less importance in trans-Atlantic economic relations; the mythology insists that it be treated reverently. Because it has such a hold on the American and European imaginations, trade policy in its broadest sense must be handled skillfully to insure that it does not contaminate the entire Atlantic well.

We must be clear on the relative substantive importance of each problem if the overall trade issue is to be dealt with intelligently. This means a precise order of priority to prevent every problem from becoming an international test of wills. A climate of good sense and a process which seeks to solve problems are only possible in an international environment of trade liberalization. Acceptance of the *status quo* or desperate national reactions to payments deficits would accelerate the slide back toward increasing international protectionism.

In the course of President Nixon's flying visit to Brussels in 1969 he announced that the Community's first Cabinet visitor would be Secretary of Commerce Maurice Stans. Genial in the fashion of a banker confronting a dubious client, Stans demonstrated a capacity to lecture and an inability to listen that would set a pattern for the visits of other Cabinet travellers. He unveiled to startled Commissioners the administration's contribution to the economic lexicon, the notion of "fair trade." While imprecise, he seemed to suggest that regardless of international rules or obligations, Washington would superimpose a further, unilaterally determined test of fairness. Many Europeans correctly read the message as an indication of more vigorous American nationalism.

A central policy question before the United States and the Community is the nature of the international trading system. As the Congress was developing trade legislation and preparations began in Tokyo in the fall of 1973 for the international negotiations, a number of basic issues remained obscure. Was there to be a strengthening or weakening of the basic notion of a multilateral system? Was the Community system of preferences a transitional phase, or did it cast the shadow of an alternative approach, regionalism, with a worldwide order distinctly peripheral? It was hard to tell, for the Europeans were adept in verbalizing the compatibility of the two and defending the association arrangements. There were disturbing undercurrents, however. We and the Europeans are so proficient in finding liberal words to justify illiberal actions that it is necessary to take a hard look at what each in fact does.

The Community ambivalently pays homage to the GATT at the same time that its policy of preferential arrangements poses the most serious threat to the multilateral system. The Europeans seem to hope that they can escape the hard choice, that somehow the GATT and preferences can continue to coexist. Although some observers see a European-African bloc emerging as an alternative to the GATT system, this has never seemed a conscious European objective. In rational terms, it would be inconsistent with European self-interest.

America's anger over the concentric circles of association arrangements is partially explained by pure frustration. The United States cannot creditably respond to the Community preferences by developing its own competitive system, say with Latin America, as suggested on various occasions by Nelson Rockefeller, Nixon, and Connally. This is a ludicrous threat, for Latin America would reject any such Yankee embrace, which in any event would not coincide with United States' interests. Other flights of rhetoric, proposals for a North Atlantic Free Trade Area, have the flavor of amateurish bluff. In reality, a world of blocs would be incompatible with the interests of any of the major economic units. Surging demands for raw materials, food and fertilizer crises, and financial upheavals imply a chaotic but single world. A system of blocs would be at exact odds with reality and the interests of all countries, quite apart from its political complexity and inherent instability.

The Community's African, Caribbean, Mediterranean, and neutral arrangements have nearly reached their limits. As long as these countries had some hope of gaining preferential status with the Community they had everything to gain from good manners. As these hopes die, the discriminatory aspects of the Community system promise to intensify the bitterness between those developing countries which are tied to the Community and those left out in the cold. Family harmony has been far from complete, even within the ranks of the associated countries; for example, Madrid charges that the Community gives Algerian oranges greater preference than those accorded to exports from Spain. In short, as the world's major trader the Community should find it hard to ignore its self-interest in strengthening the multilateral system.

Beyond the asperity of the debate, the question remains as to the depth of the disagreement over principle. As it is the custom of nations to display their finest talent in rationalizing what they have done, so the Europeans have justified and admired their association policy. Apart from this spirited defense, the association arrangements do spring from several important European interests. The northern European and Mediterranean agreements reflect basic European concern for the economic strength and political stability of those areas. Furthermore, tariff preference is one of the few instruments easily available to the still primitive

Community in achieving its political ends. Trade preferences were at hand; other means were not.

For years, Washington had used the shotgun approach, condemning all preference. Finally, as they appreciated the weakness of the frontal attack, American officials wisely narrowed their fire and concentrated on the noxious reverse preferences the Community had extracted from the developing countries. In 1973 the Europeans indicated that they would eliminate this aspect of their association agreements. The American objectives should be to stop the geographic and substantive extensions of the arrangements, to see that the Community does in fact eliminate reverse preferences, and to establish our own system of generalized preferences so that, in time, the Community arrangements can be subsumed within a universal system.

A major, long-term goal should be to move the Community away from anachronistic insistence on some tariff protection and to persuade it to accept free trade in industrial products. (Needless to say, no inconsiderable effort would be required to get the United States, first, to accept this objective.) With agreement on industrial free trade secured, the United States could live with the preferences as a transitional phenomenon which would be dissolved in the process of general liberalization. From the other side, with a little imagination Europeans could use America's interest in free trade and the dissolution of the preferential arrangements as leverage to assure that America continues to move in a liberal direction.

Success in resolving the broadest issues of economic policy, as we enter the planned international negotiations on the future of the trading system, depends on the intelligence and skill with which the smallest and meanest trade problems are managed. Experience in recent years has shown how *not* to do it. The management of these issues is an exercise in mutual responsibility: how to contain inevitable conflict; how to ease the friction which is an integral part of the working of the international economic system. In the past, trade issues have had a life and velocity of their own. Americans and Europeans felt free, perhaps even morally obligated, to increase the friction and conflict. Reform begins with an informal pact which recognizes that the tone, language, and way in which these issues are handled can be as important as their substance. This will only occur if political leaders in Europe and the United States demand it, and see that it is done. A policy of containment, restraint, and mutual compromise needs the strongest political will and close control. Such a policy will succeed only with support by both the Commission and the member states, only with common cause between the executive branch and the Congress.

A process of containment and compromise as the means for the resolution of trade problems is not conceptually difficult. In effect, it is an economic sausage factory producing an unending series of small trade-off packages between the Community and the United States. Planning the packages can best be initiated in Brussels, between the U. S. Mission and the Commission. For instance, a package might include European concession on certain tobacco taxes for American agreement to relax restrictions on selected European quality cheeses. Outline of the package and tentative agreement to explore the matter further would be entirely distinct from where and how the individual issues would eventually be negotiated; actual negotiation, for example, could be held under GATT auspices. The premise is balance and reciprocity; each side gives a little and each side gains a little.

Success depends on each side's determination to confront its own entrenched interest groups, which inevitably will resist any change in the *status quo*. If there is political commitment and control and the matter is presented as a continuing process, it may just be possible to placate or neutralize the affected domestic groups. It must be made clear that no one industry or interest group has been selected for lonely sacrifice.

Experience in recent years suggests that with the best will in the world only a minority of the individual trade issues could be solved. The optimum result of a procedure of restraint and negotiation is continued surveillance of problems to insure that they do not needlessly harm general relations. It becomes harder to make a flat-out attack against a partner's trade measure if there has been continuing discussion and if the guilty party has candidly explained the domestic pressures that led to his transgression. If an approach of this sort were adopted, it could have a singular value in improving the Atlantic atmosphere.

For years the agricultural issue has been manifestly insoluble. Pursuit of American farm interests should rest on a long-term perspective, take careful account of the forces within the Community working for modification of its policy, draw on the support of third countries with parallel interests (Canada, Australia, and Latin American states), and use the leverage of international negotiation. Major changes in the structure of the Common Agricultural Policy will come about over time, primarily in response to internal pressure and not as the result of lectures on agricultural economics. America can join forces, with some subtlety we may hope, with those Europeans who are in revolt against excessively high price levels and costly, inefficient programs. It should be possible to enlarge the areas of common interest—lower food prices for consumers, interest in food stockpiles, emphasis on meat rather than dairy production. Thus, even with respect to agriculture, perhaps the most difficult area, there are common interests to be explored.

With imagination and luck some benefit might be extracted from the soybean debacle and the humpty-dumpty world of agricultural shortages. As demands for export controls rose, the American farm community vividly realized its stake in an orderly, open international market. The Community found itself, in 1974, rather than imposing levies on cheap imports, watching world food prices rise above CAP levels. Petrus Lardinois, appointed in 1973 the commissioner responsible for agriculture, approached farm policy more flexibly and without the doctrinaire commitment of his predecessor, Mansholt. A new situation, new problems, and new people made it possible for Washington and the Community to break away from old patterns of conflict. Lardinois and Secretary of Agriculture Butz were to develop the kind of personal rapport that had entirely escaped Mansholt and Hardin. But falling farm prices along with rising tempers of farmers prevented any fundamental change in the trans-Atlantic agricultural relationship.

If there is to be reasonable Atlantic accommodation, Europeans must refrain from pressing demands on Washington when a favorable response is clearly impossible. Since 1968, first the Johnson and then the Nixon administrations wished to eliminate American Selling Price (ASP). But the situation in Congress precluded any chance of scrapping this thoroughly objectionable nontariff barrier. Through the years, the Europeans pressed the issue of the Kennedy Round ASP protocol. Time ran out in early 1973 and the protocol was killed. The Community action was emotionally comprehensible, but hardly calculated to strengthen the hands of liberal forces in the United States—or even to serve longer-term European interests.

Within the philosophical framework of dealing continuously with trade issues as a common problem, the two sides of the Atlantic could develop a procedure for a joint attack on nontariff barriers (NTBs), an area for future trade struggles. Using private as well as governmental analyses, such as studies by the OECD High Level Group and GATT studies, the Community and the United States could agree to continuing, informal exchange on how to cope with this increasingly difficult subject. This would be supplementary to any results from the major GATT negotiation, which, at the most, will deal with a few NTBs and perhaps reach some agreement for future work in the area. The management and elimination of these restrictions, however, must also be seen in the context of Community-American relations. As in the case of ASP, many of the barriers will yield only to bilateral negotiation between the Community and the United States. In view of the firm grip Congress will keep on NTBs, balanced agreements between the United States and the Community, involving several items on each side, could be a prerequisite to American legislative acquiescence. As in the procedure for negotiating trade packages, the distinction must be maintained between exploration, assessment of the importance of various restrictions and ways of getting at these problems, and actual negotiation. For instance, in certain areas where Community and American practice and policy are similar—anti-dumping, countervailing duties, and standards—it may be possible to envision a harmonization of policies.

The export embargo of mid-1973 was not an isolated agricultural phenomenon, but presaged a new field for Atlantic and international conflict—raw materials. With inflation the dominating issue for all governments, shortages of critical materials which led to skyrocketing prices induced domestic pressures for unilateral export restriction. By 1974, as the world economy faltered, speculation about international cooperation was replaced by a common fear that the industrialized countries, in their struggle to survive, would be driven to totally destructive competition. One looked in vain for the willingness to sacrifice which had marked the immediate postwar period.

Cooperation, the Indispensable Ingredient

Emphasis on expanding areas of cooperation between the Community and the United States derives from Jean Monnet's philosophy that progress comes from the common attack on a common problem, rather than the pitched battle of adversaries over divisive issues. The notion of a relationship rooted in cooperation is neither contrived nor quixotic.

Washington's proposal for the OECD High Level Group to explore trade policy, for instance, contemplated American-Community cooperation within a small expert committee. The idea lost its luster when the United States forgot the essence of its original approach, namely to establish an independent group of nongovernmental "wise men." Instead, Washington appointed William Eberle, who was designated the President's Special Trade Representative.

As the work unfolded in Paris, Ambassador Eberle was a source of constant confusion—when was he speaking as an expert and when was he negotiating for the United States? The Community countered by naming as its expert Theodorus Hijzen, the Commission's experienced and tough Kennedy Round negotiator. The two sides were off to the races. Occasional efforts to create an atmosphere of informality and candid exchange between Washington and Brussels aborted. In his periodic sessions with Commission officials Eberle sought intimate dialogue, but the injection of heavy-handed bargaining ploys into informal discussions and his propensity for giving previews or post-mortems of his arguments to the press destroyed whatever chance he might have had. Until the administration submitted its trade legislation to the Congress in early 1973, admittedly he had a nasty assignment; America had no foreign economic policy or strategy. Eberle appeared to hope that American trade policy would somehow emerge from frantic discussions in Europe. Europeans entirely missed this interpretation of his activities and saw only another American Dr. Jekyll and Mr. Hyde.

There is a moral to be extracted from this unhappy period. Without a clear American policy for conducting relations with the Community in a framework of intimate cooperation, supported by officials who have the capacity to win the confidence of the Europeans, the trans-Atlantic alternative will be continual conflict, argument, and misunderstanding. The approach can go either way—cooperation or confrontation—but whichever it is, the process will be habit-forming. When senior agricultural officials struck the sour note, their subordinates quickly picked up the tune. The converse is also true. Where a spirit of cooperation prevailed between the environmental experts from Washington and people with similar responsibilities in the Commission, for instance, this set a pattern for a more constructive approach by other officials whose normal life-style was trans-Atlantic badgering.

The United States-Euratom Joint Program offers lessons for the future.

Cooperation in this endeavor began in the 1950s, well before the Euratom Treaty was signed. The work brought the staff of the Atomic Energy Commission and European officials into close and continual contact at all levels. The potentiality for dispute has always been as real in this field as in any other; but, through the extensive experience of joint action, the continuity in relations between American and European industry, and the close rapport between competent, informed Americans and Europeans, a climate of cooperation developed and persisted.

Advocacy of cooperation and a common strategy raises at once the cry of duplication or conflict with the international system; for example, with the rules and the GATT procedures for dealing with trade matters. It should be evident that the Community and the United States share the objective that the global arrangements must be strengthened, not weakened, and that a primary purpose of trans-Atlantic cooperation is to reinforce the international system.

The issue raised is especially difficult, for it is layered with both real and specious arguments. American and European vows of loyalty and allegiance to the GATT have an air of sanctimony. GATT rules and procedures have been employed more as tools to attack and defend specific cases than to build an international institution and a solid body of economic law. And the crippling disease of the United Nations has spread to the GATT—the use of the institution as a platform for propaganda and the insidious practice, by those with the votes and a majority, of overriding both the letter and the intent of the basic agreement. As we have seen, the Community, conscious of the power derived from its preferential agreements and the ambitions of those seeking such arrangements, finds it hard to resist the temptation of employing this voting strength to serve immediate ends.

In the Community the French have used the GATT issue with subtle effectiveness. They would press on their colleagues the presumed GATT implications of issues in order to frustrate those member states wishing to collaborate more closely with the United States. The French lived in the fear that direct United States-Community negotiations would lead to unbalanced European trade concessions to the Americans. The emphasis on GATT gave them some assurance of reciprocity. They would raise the specter of the Third World's anger should Europe dilute its GATT engagement by bilateral trade cooperation with America. As with all imaginative demagoguery, this tactic involved the adept blending of some substance with much emotion. It was also the sort of argument which would throw the Community into vast confusion, resulting in general support for the French position.

Behind the Community's debating points lie real problems. Increasingly, the trade policy interests of the industrial countries differ from those of the developing countries. The danger to GATT as an institution arises from its failure to deal with problems of the major industrial countries. The unfortunate trend is to admit defeat and permit the GATT to go the way of the United Nations through cynical use or disuse. Far from intensifying the problems of the GATT, real European-American cooperation in dealing with Atlantic trade problems and an honest commitment to strengthening the institution could be its salvation.

An additional means of dealing with the bilateral-multilateral dilemma is further use of the OECD. The trade work of the OECD has always been less than meets the eye. But if the Community can establish itself as a political entity in the OECD, certain trade matters of concern to the Community and the United States could be brought into this forum, or even initiated there. Once issues of primary interest to the industralized countries have been considered in the OECD, they could subsequently be brought within the GATT ambit to give them sanction and to provide the basis for future enforcement, coincidentally strengthening the GATT.

International conflict and bitter disagreements are in prospect if there is no system to establish the facts of disputed issues, with agreement by contending parties to accept the fact-finding procedure. After three days of intensive exchange with Brussels officials in 1972, members of the House Ways and Means Committee concluded that the roots of many Atlantic problems lay in differing data, statistics, and in the absence of any method for reconciling these basic disagreements. The GATT could be made to fill this vacuum, but only if the United States and the Europeans wish it to do so and are prepared to assure it the necessary resources. If the Atlantic nations and Japan do not move in this direction, the Philadelphia lawyers of trade disputes will continue to produce their own self-serving analyses and data which "prove" whatever case is in their clients' interests.

In international economic affairs the danger is anarchy even more than rampant protectionism. Yet suggestions for common American-

Community action elicit a double-edged criticism: First, such collaboration carries the risk of degeneration into some exclusive, inner-oriented Atlantic arrangements, including sly collusion against the interests of others; second, despite the most impeccable motives and evident good works, a suspicious, resentful Third World will always think the worst, convinced that Atlantic cooperation is synonymous with the incestuous behavior of the wealthy nations, intent on protecting themselves at the expense of the poor. On the other hand, if there is no American-European collaboration the only real alternative, confrontation, will destroy the international system and quite possibly plunge the world, third countries included, into economic anarchy.

But the need for cooperation extends beyond the Atlantic area. Common endeavor by the United States, the European Community, and Japan is essential to any viable international order—the point is as obvious as is the way it has been ignored. The issue transcends the positive, reciprocal benefits of collaboration or of avoiding damaging disputes. The three must recognize their responsibilities to one another and, as three, to the world at large. It is difficult to know which of the three blunders the most. Each in its own way has seemed determined to worsen an already bad situation.

The full dimensions of Japan's insularity were manifested in the insensitivity to the economic and psychological consequences of its mercantilist policies on its major partners, and the threat its actions posed to the international economic system which contributed so much to Japanese prosperity. In another of those unique and startling reversals of directions, by 1973 Japan had first revalued and then floated the yen, reduced or eliminated most of its trade restrictions to the point where the Japanese could be described as the most liberal of the three major trading entities, and was progressing rapidly in opening the country to foreign investment. The Japanese "way" of stubborn resistance to change, new consensus, and then reversal meant that they were to receive little credit for their new, responsible policies. The shock of the 1974 fuel crisis, with the cost of oil an extra $9 billion a year, left Japan with its foreign and economic policies in shambles. There was no sudden conversion to international cooperation; instead, Japan took a page from Europe's book on Arab appeasement—collaboration among consumers might provoke the suppliers.

The Nixon administration's handling of Japan was a case study in diplomatic incompetence, from brandishing the Trading with the Enemy Act as a device for extracting textile concessions to callous indifference to Japanese sensibilities in the dramatic unfolding of the Peking spectacular. European policy toward Japan has likewise been free of enlightenment. Limited direct contact and European inactivity account for the fact that little overt wrong has been done. But European inclinations and prejudices run from ignoring Japan to the imposition of further restrictions. In his April 23, 1973, speech Kissinger had inserted, backhandedly, a call to Europe for the inclusion of Japan in Atlantic councils. The idea fell stillborn among the Europeans. Late in the year there was a curious European initiative, consistent with the pervasive incompetence of diplomacy in 1973. The Japanese were invited to join in the preparation of a bilateral European-Japanese declaration, presumably patterned on the statement being developed by the nine in response to Kissinger's April appeal. The Japanese were inscrutable and unresponsive; the Americans, furious.

As Japanese exports and their balance of payments exploded in the 1960s, American frustration and anger ricocheted against the Europeans. It was consistent with the general search for scapegoats on which to saddle American's ills to complain that European restrictions against Japanese goods forced Japan to concentrate on the American market. Mixed with this conviction of Europe's complicity was a tinge of envy for its cleverness in protecting itself. Washington would reiterate its demand that the Europeans "share the burden" of Japanese imports.

The trilateral relationship will not develop without America's leadership since the Japanese-European dialogue is nonexistent. The Japanese would not presume to plan and execute a policy of United States-European Community-Japanese cooperation; nor would Europe respond to such initiatives with anything but suspicion. Yet there have been signs of Japanese willingness to cooperate, even to look for ways of mediating disputes between the United States and the European Community. This sensitivity and flexibility could be put to use if a way were found to move the Europeans. Asia is low on any European list of priorities, with Japan near the bottom. In addition to cultural differences, Europe's fear of the Japanese economy, the geographic factor, differing security interests and commitments are stubborn obstacles to trilateral cooperation. In its call for a new Atlantic Charter, Washington ran head-on into a problem which ruled out a single document: NATO versus the Community. The disparity was even more acute for Japan, a country totally outside the Atlantic security framework, whose defense policy was a mixture of home forces and dependence on the United States.

It would be nice if someone other than the United States would take the lead. America had sullied its reputation and raised serious question for the Japanese about its reliability. Kissinger, who had become for them the agent and symbol of callous America, was hardly the Secretary of State to erase the accumulated grievances. And Europeans found further reason to resist collaboration with Japan. Behind America's protestations of noble purpose, the Europeans thought they detected the real purpose: to use the trilateral concept as a means of shifting Europe into the United States' uncomfortable role as the prime target for Japanese exports.

Should the Community and the United States intensify their collaboration, the implications for relations with Japan must be considered. With 1975 as a point of departure, it will be infeasible for several years to expect the expansion of the kind of intimate cooperation suggested earlier with Japan as a coequal partner. Emotionally, philosophically, and politically, the Europeans are unprepared for such cooperation. For those Europeans with mixed feelings about closer Atlantic cooperation—some fearful perhaps of American dominance, others of a spasmodic revival of Kissinger bullying—proposals for Japanese inclusion in Community-American endeavors can be used to shoot down any ideas for cooperation whatsoever. If headway is to be made, however, the realities of European and Japanese opinion and policy must be accepted. In private conversations Japanese officials familiar with Europe speculate about less formal, transitional arrangements. For example, the United States and the Community might begin to work on a given problem, but before the two reached agreement on a possible course of action the matter would be explored with the Japanese to see whether they might be involved. As a permanent arrangement this smacks of discrimination; as an interim device it fits within the narrow parameters of existing American-Europeans-Japanese realities—and prejudices.

If there is any chance at all for a policy of cooperation among the three, the President of the United States must take the lead, and the policy must be carried forward with the governmental discipline more typical of the British civil service than the traditional bureaucratic license of Washington agencies. The problem will not be solved by some simple, dramatic action, but only by continuing, persistent pressure. Modest measures can help the process along; for instance, informal but regular contacts in Brussels of the European Commissioners and the Japanese and American ambassadors to the Community and parallel, similarly informal, discussions in Washington. The primary purpose would be to generate the habit of candid consultation among the three. To be effective, the initiative would have to be taken by the United States, at the level of the Deputy Secretary of State.

In light of the European attitudes, the most that could be expected of the Japanese or European representatives in the short run would be to accept an invitation to talk. It is not a lost cause. As a result of the multiple crises of the early 1970s and the patient work of enlightened private groups, the three began to be aware of their collective interests. The Japanese, for example, became less wooden in meetings with Americans and Europeans; the Westerners, more sensitive to Japanese mores. After years of temporizing, the Commission fought through the Council of Ministers a proposal to establish a modest Community information office in Tokyo; when faced by Japan's obvious dissatisfaction, the matter was considered again and agreement finally reached on a full-fledged mission to Japan, similar to the one in Washington.

Beyond Immediate Controversies

Containing and resolving disputes through cooperation is curative medicine. The preventive medicine is a deliberate policy of cooperation on issues which are not sources of present conflict. The specific examples which follow, concerning environment, energy, restrictive business practices, and the Third World, are offered as illustrations, not as a comprehensive outline of all that should or can be done.

Unfortunately, failure in the past to make any noticeable progress along this positive track has been due primarily to European reticence. In many areas Community decisions have not been taken, and Commission representatives have found themselves unable to respond to American initiatives; in others, the responsibility for the subject remains within the competence of the member governments. The summit meeting in 1972 began to push against the boundaries of the Community. But the problem of enlargement, then "renegotiation," and the unsettled question of Community competence effectively prevented the Community from being a partner ready to engage actively in new substantive areas. A prerequisite to effective cooperation is a Commission sure of its domestic footing.

American efforts at cooperation with the Community in collateral economic fields were severely restricted during the Gaullist era by the European doctrinal dispute over the Community's powers. Where the treaties gave it no specific mandate, French logic insisted that the Community as such lacked authority and could not act. This reservation seemed artful to Americans raised on a doctrine of implied powers and eager to "do something" about evident problems. Furthermore, especially in new areas such as environment or energy, the Commission, woefully short on experts, found it almost impossible to match the quantity and variety of talent that Washington could produce. The initiative must come from Washington, and it will require high-level supervision to assure its close attunement to the complicated Community structure. While the Washington scene is free of the intricate constitutional problems of the Community, the American bureaucracy has its own peculiarities. Nothing so stimulates the bureaucratic hormones as claims for jurisdiction over new, glamorous programs. These battles for supremacy limit the scant attention of most Washington officials for the international implications of their actions. This domestic preoccupation and general innocence of foreign affairs was notable in the early months of William Simon's tour as energy czar. Later, naturally enough, when the dust of battle has settled, the excitement of foreign travel and international conferences will take over. But whether the field of possible Atlantic cooperation is new or old, nothing useful will happen unless the responsible domestic agency takes the initiative and organizes a continuing effort. While the White House and the Department of State can prod, monitor, and give political advice, discreetly if possible, in the final analysis cooperation will depend on the active interest and initiative of the domestic departments.

Cooperation in environmental matters illustrates the complexity of the relationship between the Community and member states. The sheer congestion of Europe pushes the continent toward some Community approach, but the immediate reaction to ecological problems is primarily national, with the Community's responsibility limited and obscure. National governments have the advantage of ministries, staff, and money. The experienced European bureaucrat, too, has an unerring instinct to lay hold of the new field—and the resources and power that go with it. Stimulated by NATO's identification of environmental problems, for example, European governments moved quickly to establish bilateral working relations with the U.S. Department of Transportation, the Environmental Protection Agency, and others. Had Washington adopted any clear policy of support for Community as contrasted with *ad hoc* bilateral arrangements, it still would have been self-defeating to interfere in these essential relations, or to press directly for some superior Community-United States framework, no matter how logical or desirable. The middle ground is close, informal contact between the Commission, on behalf of the Community, and the American authorities to insure that there is reasonable balance between the Community and the national, bilateral relationships. In this delicate area of intra-European politics and bureaucracy the Americans can do no better than move as far and as fast as the Commission recommends. On the other hand, even the most discreet Commission initiatives stir up indignant reactions from national bureaucracies, for member state officials rightly regard the Community as the enemy of the *status quo*.

The handling of this relationship by Russell Train, Director of the Environmental Protection Agency, was exemplary—careful, sensitive, and cooperative. He took the Commission officials into his confidence, outlining his plans and the policies he hoped to see adopted by the administration and the Congress. If the Europeans were interested, he was prepared to make available pertinent working papers. It would be hard to overestimate the psychological value of discussing issues with Europe when the United States is still feeling its way and before national policy has hardened. There is the soothing effect of shared ignorance and indecision.

Antitrust policy and the need to cope with restrictive business practices suggest cooperation of a different sort. In this area the Community has clear but limited statutory authority; it is one of the few fields of independent Commission power. Furthermore, both the United States and the Community are groping their way in a murky economic area where neither the problems nor the solutions are simple. The certainty in distinguishing between good and evil, characteristic of the Sherman Act and of the days of Thurman Arnold, has disappeared, with no consensus about the economic and social tests to be applied. In this situation, intellectual exchange could benefit equally the Community and the United

States as each attempts to determine the policies most likely to deal equitably with both the general public and the business interests.

The practice of informal and useful discussions between the Antitrust Division of the U.S. Department of Justice and Commission officials has developed over the years. The natural fraternity among "trust-busters" stems from appreciation of industry's use of the alleged freedom from restraint of its competitors as an argument for relaxing domestic antitrust laws and regulations. Everyone gains—regulator, company, and the public—from harmonization of policy and regulation. In addition, a procedure for regular, informal exchange between the Justice Department, the Federal Trade Commission, the State Department, and the Commission authorities has the further merit of stimulating a common strategy against the importuning, and potentially collusive, action by certain American and European firms.

Close contact between Brussels and Washington minimizes the risk of one side's surprising the other. In 1969 the Justice Department moved without warning or explanation against British Petroleum, which sought to buy into the east coast gasoline distribution system. Reaction in Europe to the antitrust action was quick and emotional. The Europeans were convinced the American objective was simply to thwart a foreign purchase of American property. The search by the European press for drama and hidden motives centered quickly on the allegation that this was an example of rampant American nationalism. A mirror image of this phenomenon was Continental Can's three-year embroilment with the Commission's restrictive practices division. Americans openly wondered if the charge against Continental Can of "abuse of a dominant position" was not in fact a thinly veiled attack by the Community against a large, multinational American company.

The policies of the Community and the United States toward the developing world could be either another area for cooperation or an arena for further controversy. Despite America's present and past role as a major dispenser of aid and its position as the largest market for Third World products, the absolute and relative decline in the level of its assistance and the evidence of fading American interest in the broad problem of development have contributed to a growing resentment in those countries. The poor nations bitterly chafed under the application of the U.S. surtax on imports in the aftermath of the August 1971 crisis, because, as deficit countries, they could see no economic reason for penalizing the goods they export. Washington only fanned the resentment by its opposition to suggestions that Special Drawing Rights (SDRs) be distributed to the developing countries.

The Community, spared its own ITT case, applied no surtax, and furthermore showed a certain interest in the distribution of SDRs. The long-term European embrace of commodity agreements as a device for shoring-up prices for raw materials and evening out wide cyclical swings made it easy in 1974 for the Community, in a far more volatile supply-and-demand situation, to propose to the associated states new arrangements for many raw materials to assure higher-than-market prices and stable returns to the producers. America, on the other hand, has identified itself in the minds of the developing countries as flatly opposed to such agreements. And Washington's doctrinaire objections to preferential arrangements between the Community and the associated states were construed as gratuitous interference in a relationship deemed valuable by the poor countries.

In a perverse way the Community benefits from the sorry American performance. The Europeans still seem to care; by 1973, aid as a percentage of GNP was three times that of the United States; in 1971 the Community had put in place a generalized preference scheme; and its association agreements were of tangible benefit to the poorer countries. Many observers in the Third World thought Europe sensitive and responsive to their plight, in contrast to a less interested America, inclined to withdraw from international responsibility.

A Community-American dialogue on the subjects of levels of assistance, multilateral versus bilateral aid, and generalized preferences could improve the performance of both sides. Such collaboration may be essential to revive lagging American interest. The pressure on exhaustible raw materials and the mounting impatience of the producing countries, stimulated by dramatic bargaining successes of the Arab states, create an entirely new international environment. There is an uneasy sense that the panoply of accumulated assistance programs may not be attuned to the changed political and economic relationship between producing and consuming countries.

The stage has been set for rivalry and competition between the United States and the Community over the explosive demand for raw materials, the role of private investment and the multinational company in extractive, processing and marketing industries, and differing degrees of sensitivity to the impact of labor-intensive manufactured goods such as textiles. In addition to the differences in approach cited, there are other forces at work within Europe which could cause the Community to set itself self-consciously apart from America in this area. As Europe's hopes for economic equality died, battered by Kissinger's heavy-handed diplomacy and by Europe's own internal divisions, condemned to dependence on America's nuclear weapons and conventional forces for its defense, the answers to these frustrations could be sought in independent Community policies toward the Third World, even by subtle exploitation of the animus of the developing countries toward the United States. In an Atlantic atmosphere of indifference and contention, with communication faulty, all of the elements exist which could convert this into an area of dangerous Atlantic controversy.

Energy could have been one of the subjects for common action. For years, American experts assumed that the Europeans would see the necessity for a Community energy policy. A crisis which by 1972 seemed inevitable to many Americans was ignored across the Atlantic; and energy remained a source of division, jealousy, and confusion to the Europeans. Although the Commission grasped the dimensions of the problem and the need for a Community approach, it encountered stubborn resistance from both the member states and the European oil industry. A gifted, energetic State Department official, James Akins, launched a largely personal effort to engage the Community in joint exploration of this long-range Atlantic problem: estimates of future demand and supply, sharing of shortages in crisis situations, research and development of new sources of energy, special projects such as nuclear tankers, and relations with the oil-producing states. But by 1974, when energy was no longer a problem but a crisis, it had enveloped all aspects of Atlantic life. Once the pre-crisis opportunity was lost, the quiet, continuing staff relationship envisioned by Akins and Fernand Spaak, the Commission's Director-General for Energy, was beyond resurrection. Again, the primary obstacle to American-Community cooperation was Europe itself—its inability to agree on the rudiments of Community energy policy and disagreement on the role, if any, of Community institutions. Despite the fortuitous departure of Pompidou and Jobert in early 1974, the Europeans continued to flounder.

As the crisis ramified, the kind of Atlantic cooperation which had appeared eminently sensible became more and more unlikely. For years,

Walter Levy and other experts had warned of the inequities and dangers in a situation where the producing states engaged themselves in an effective cartel, OPEC, and the consumers stumbled about alone, each day more vulnerable to the Arab suppliers. If the advice that the consumers organize themselves had been followed when first proffered and before the producers had become impassioned by the 1973 war and conscious of the full power of their monopolistic position, a balanced and equitable relationship might have been painlessly established between consumers and producers. It could also have saved Europe from the agonies of the divisive classification imposed by the Arabs on European countries as "friends, neutrals, and enemies."

The energy crisis was an unmitigated disaster for the Atlantic nations, all cost and no benefit. At the height of the embargo Europeans and Americans alike were ready to make personal sacrifices. But harried leaders lacked the vision and the nerve. As the embargo eased, Micawber became the patron saint of the Atlantic governments. Europe and America temporized alone and together. Considerations of long-term remedies became debates among experts with action and painful choices deferred. Those Europeans who hoped that the crisis would finally galvanize the Community out of its lethargy were to be disappointed. What remained were the scars of the war, memories of ugly recrimination, and accumulating, unsolved economic problems. In the future the Atlantic nations would be wise to anticipate such crises, to develop contingency plans, and to have in place the kind of close staff relationship Akins and Spaak had futilely urged.

The new International Energy Agency (IEA) provided the only relief in this dreary vista. For the moment narrow nationalistic responses were set aside. The agreement imposed far-reaching obligations on its members—development of new sources of energy, stand-by arrangements in the event of future shortages, a "safety-net" to deal with the financial implications of the crisis. Worry about what might lie ahead in no way diminishes this substantial accomplishment. Some congressional reaction was critical, with reservation expressed about the contribution to the financial "safety-net," and rejection of any American responsibility to come to the "aid of the Europeans." In light of the nationalistic mood, others wondered, if another emergency occurred, whether the country would meet its IEA commitment to share its dwindling reserves. Europeans were asking similar questions. Would they have the political will to live up to the terms of the agreement? Once again the Community was the odd man out. Only after issues had been resolved within the IEA framework would the Community agree on its own limited energy policies. French refusal to join the agency made matters worse. The chance to use the energy crisis as a means of strengthening the Community had been lost, first, by the Europeans, but abetted by American indifference.

The United States cannot escape the responsibility for formulating the broad economic relationship it wishes to have with the Community. There is too much dry tinder about. The energy-financial crisis magnified old problems, such as the badly battered financial system, and added a range of new international issues. In addition to the friction of everyday relations, the imminent trade negotiations will release the combative instincts which are part of this kind of international contest. In fact, by almost any measurement, the opportunities for sustained economic conflict outweigh the chances of reversing course and developing the Atlantic cooperation which each side allegedly wants. Therefore, it is all the more urgent for Washington to mount a new effort to define the common goals, devise policies to achieve them, and ensure that the American government marches together and in one direction.

Chapter VII

Political Relations

Europeans insist that their goal is political, but quarrel when they come to define it. It is commonplace to construe "political" as synonymous with foreign policy. In fact, as applied to today's Europe, the term must include such sensitive areas as agriculture and certainly the institutional development of the Community. American interest in European political ambitions includes the domestic and institutional as well as the foreign policy aspects. A policy of imaginative support for the Community—appreciation of European motives and actions, a re-emphasis on American interest in the process, and deliberate steps to bring the Community and the United States into closer harmony—cannot avoid calculated encouragement of the Community's political development.

The ebb and flow of Community activity in this area has been dramatic. At the end of 1972 the heads-of-government reiterated brave slogans, identified political goals and problems, and laid out a work program. Pressures mounted on governments to do more than talk about political union. It had become evident that monetary union was impossible without movement at the political level, progressive but discreet delegation of national sovereignty, closely coordinated member state budgetary and fiscal policies—in particular far more effective Community institutions. As *Ostpolitik* lost momentum, Willy Brandt took the lead in stressing the importance of Western Europe and the Community. In his inaugural appearance at the United Nations Brandt stated in unequivocal terms the prospect of a "European state" by the end of the decade. Without intent, the Nixon administration pushed the Europeans along. The backing and filling about the "Year of Europe" and focus on the Declaration of Principles left the nine no alternative but to get together, as they had been forced to do in connection with the negotiations in the Conference on Security and Cooperation in Europe.

The European Parliament was also stirring with the prospect of greater influence, exercising the powers it had, and clamoring for more. The Commission labored to recover some of its authority. But at the center of the Community would remain the Council of Ministers, the instrument of political power for the member states.

In lieu of Heath's commitment to political union, the Wilson government was outspokenly hostile, a matter of socialist principle for some and of devious tactics for others. Oddly enough, although "political unity" stuck in the British throat, member governments found discussion of political issues, even the search for political consensus, a pleasant escape from the contentious economic business of the Community that impinged directly on the internal interests of each country. In the event, 1974 was the year of "renegotiation," with European attention further diverted as political matters sank from sight before the rising tide of inflation. Despite these startling shifts, the pull of political union remained. It could be seen in the surprised satisfaction with which the Europeans found themselves working together in connection with the Copenhagen declaration, the Conference on European Security, and the Mutual and Balanced Force Reductions (MBFR) negotiations. New habits of political coordination were being formed.

A Community Foreign Policy?

Foreign policy will test the political will of the Community. From the Fouchet Plan of the Gaullist days to the Davignon Committee, the lack of progress can be laid to both substantive and organizational obstacles. The Community's political ambitions became ensnared early in sharp disagreement among the member states on the relationship of the proposed political work to the Community as defined by the Treaty of Rome and on the nature, role, and physical location of the political secretariat—whether it should be in Paris, as Pompidou demanded, or in Brussels with the other Community institutions. At first blush the French insistence on Paris seemed little more than a frivolous grab for patronage. In fact, the French position was serious and designed to affect significantly the future development of the Community. If the political work could be separated from the economic and be located apart from the Brussels institutions, the latter would be weakened, and the new political activities would be more easily subject to member state control. In addition, a decision to establish the political secretariat in Paris, geographically and spiritually apart from Brussels, would perpetuate the nonpolitical and technical image of the Community and place another obstacle in the way of rational institutional development.

The function of gathering intelligence presents a similar problem in which procedure and substance intermingle. The conduct of foreign affairs requires an elaborate, worldwide system to gather and digest information of a confidential character. Even close allies are cautious about the exchange of such intelligence, with transactions conducted in an atmosphere of elegant horse trading; information is given in order to get information. The Community approaches the field naked; it has neither the missions abroad, the experts, nor the accumulated files. The contrast with the economic area, where the Commission has trade and financial experts with experience and proven competence, is striking. A system has evolved with political directors from the member states, under the aegis of the Davignon Committee, meeting independently of the formal Community institutions. Foreign office experts produce the staff work, drawing on the resources of their national bureaucracies. Members of the Davignon Committee have developed strong fraternal ties, a significant bond in view of the unstructured, tentative nature of foreign policy coordination among the nine. Since bureaucrats are ever mindful of their prerogatives it must be assumed that this cozy arrangement among diplomatic establishments will be found to have great durability. It is not a group likely to be interested in the development of some new, even partially independent political staff; it certainly would be cool to any acquisition of this function by an enlarged European Commission. When a political secretariat is created, it will be in the mold of traditional international staffs, more administrative than substantive, more docile than assertive.

To have an authentic foreign policy the Community must find the answers to three questions of increasing difficulty. The first, the aspect that absorbs European attention, is the development of Community positions on selected subjects—the Middle East, the Mediterranean, and the elaboration of Community positions vis-à-vis the Conference on European Security. This is a policy-planning function, the distillation of expert wisdom which is passed along to those with authority to decide and act. The products are staff papers, to be used or ignored, as the ministers wish.

The second aspect is the decision-making process, presumably by the foreign ministers, which involves discussion, modification, and perhaps ultimate adoption of a policy paper. This process of national compromise, running comment, and, inevitably, premature public disclosure takes a heavy toll in substance and clarity. Brilliant foreign policy has never thrived on the committee diet. European diplomacy at this virtuoso level is beyond the reach of nine ministers gathered together in occasional meetings; perhaps it is even beyond their ambition.

Once the foreign ministers reach a decision, they face the third and more difficult part of the process: execution and negotiation. This poses a dilemma for a Europe which wants to speak with one voice. Who is to decide what the "one voice" will say, and who is to be the "voice"? More important, at least more agonizing, is the requirement that others remain silent while the "voice" speaks. The aftermath of the Copenhagen declaration on relations with the United States illustrated both the Community's achievement and its problems. It fell to the Dane, one of the foreign ministers least experienced in Community affairs, to present and presumably negotiate the decision of the nine with the United States. Kissinger's lack of enthusiasm for the procedure was marked. He consistently made clear his preference for dealing individually, and as he chose, with other foreign ministers rather than with the designee of the nine.

The Community has largely side-stepped these questions and relied on its familiar technique of the rotating presidency of the Council of Ministers, using as spokesman the representative of whatever country happens to be in the chair. This is the committee system *ad absurdum*. With eight colleagues looking over his shoulder, each confident he could handle the matter better, the Community's spokesman can be little more than the Council's designated puppet. Only blind luck would find the most competent official in charge of negotiations. And ability has no correlation with size; Gaston Thorn, as Luxembourg's Foreign Minister, demonstrated competence and vision considerably beyond that of many of his colleagues. The final question is whether any member state will commit itself to accept the results of negotiations prepared and conducted in this fashion.

Beyond the structural difficulties, the perceptions and national interests of the member states differ. Bonn's relationship with East Germany and its interest in the continuity of America's defense commitment are different from the national interests of France or Ireland. Progress in the development of a Community foreign policy places demands on the Europeans exceeding those they have encountered in the past. The political will must be there, a sense of community, and a willingness to subordinate certain national interests in order to achieve a European consensus which the Europeans insist they want.

The American Response

Determined American cooperation with the Community requires a conscious political act; to stress cooperation would also counterbalance the normal fixation on economic problems. This process involves thinking of the Community in institutional terms and as a whole—not merely the Commission and the Council of Ministers, but the European Parliament and the Court, too. America has largely ignored the constitutional structure of the Community, which has seemed to Washington as mystifying as the Tibetan theocracy. The easy and probably the most damaging response is to dismiss the Community institutions as another faceless bureaucracy, leaving relations to one's own civil servants, with contacts at the political level casual and occasional. Here recent history is instructive.

In 1969, after months of painstaking preparation and a formal invitation from President Nixon, Jean Rey, the President of the Commission, set out for Washington. On arrival at National Airport, Rey was informed that the appointment with the President had been cancelled. No plausible reason was ever given for this insult. Several White House aides offered incompetence as the excuse and suggested that a new administration had to be allowed a gaffe or two. Another rationale for the episode demonstrated the administration's combination of innocence and ignorance. Emile van Lennep, head of the OECD, by coincidence was in the capital at the same time. It was argued that it would be impolite for the President to receive the head of one "European economic organization" and not the other.

The lack of embarrassment by the White House over the collapse of the Rey visit compounded the blunder. It was the administration's good fortune that, thanks to Rey's personal stature, devotion to American-

Community relations, and sense of priorities, he refused to take personal umbrage and privately insisted to his colleagues that the Commission deflate the issue. This sorry affair contrasts with the elegant reception by the Eisenhower administration of the Community executives in June, 1959. Hallstein, Hirsch, and Finet, heads of the then three Community bodies, were installed at Blair House; and their Washington program was designed to enhance the standing of the European representatives and, through them, of the embryonic Community.

At least the Nixon administration could not be charged with discrimination: all Commissioners were treated with equal remoteness. Dr. Ralf Dahrendorf, an eminent German sociologist and until 1973 the European Commissioner in charge of foreign affairs, had known Henry Kissinger well in their earlier incarnations as academics. Despite Dahrendorf's Community responsibilities, the history of personal friendship, and a number of delicate overtures, this channel of communication never developed. The Europeans drew the obvious conclusion from the lack of interest on the part of the White House.

The visit to Washington in October 1973 of President Ortoli was a success, but not because of the preparations, which were similar to those for his predecessors—reluctance of the White House to set a date, quibbling over who had invited whom, delay in the public announcement. The latter smacked of stupidity, for once an official visit had been determined, the psychological advantages should not have been dissipated by mismanagement. The meeting with President Nixon, however, and long discussions with Kissinger and other administration officials provided the opportunity for each side to take stock of the other. Ortoli, a new President leading a new and expanded Commission, was able to determine at first hand the problems Europe had in its relations with the United States.

The plea that attention be given the Commission needs explanation. It carries no implication that the traditional relations with the nine governments be ignored. Quite apart from the extensive day-to-day bilateral business on other matters, there is important Community work to be done with the member states. But emphasis on the Commission is essential to redress the balance. The Commission, denied the most elementary trappings of government, is regarded as the poor relation both by the member governments and by Washington.

The enduring influence of bilateralism both in Europe and in America was evident in the painstaking evolution of the Community's mission in Washington. Member states were reluctant to establish more than a limited information office. To do so might detract from the role of the national embassies and in any event make their diplomatic lives more complicated, to say nothing of enhancing the Commission. It was argued that the economic and financial staffs of the several diplomatic missions could handle whatever Community business had to be taken up with the American authorities. The six, then the nine, commercial counsellors thus played out a minor tragi-comedy, calling at the State Department or the Treasury to speak *en masse* for the Community. Obduracy of France, but not France alone, for years frustrated efforts to assign an ambassador as head of the Commission's Washington mission, thus undermining the efforts of those American officials who wished to deal with the Community as a nascent political entity. Sir Christopher Soames partially finessed this obstacle with the assignment of Jens Otto Krag to Washington in the fall of 1973. Krag's political prestige was such as to make the title "ambassador" less consequential. The appointment was tangible evidence of Europe's interest in improving Community-American communication.

Europe's years of ambivalence about relations with America had worked against the interests of its own Community, at the same time unintentionally strengthening the hands of the bilateralists in Washington. The momentum of customary practice, the reflex behavior of national governments, and the Nixon administration's special taste for bilateral diplomacy left little room for a struggling Community. Attention to this political nuance was the State Department's unique responsibility. Under Rogers it lacked the muscle; under Kissinger it had the muscle, but not the will.

The Mechanics of the Relationship

The mechanics of organization produce either intense boredom or excitement in the presence of the true elixir. No matter the inspiration which goes into the formulation of policy or the determination of the political masters to carry it out, the success of the policy is dependent on the government's organization and procedures to achieve agreed ends.

This point is especially significant with respect to America's relations with the European Community. United States policy obviously involves the activities of several departments whose contacts with a growing Community will steadily expand. Somehow these interests and these contacts must be coordinated. If they are not, there will be bedlam; if they are, there is the chance that American interests may be advanced.

The move of Henry Kissinger to the State Department, on the face of it, altered dramatically the distribution of power within the government. For the first time in four years, the Department had the chance to perform its coordinating role, if the Secretary were to wish it and were willing to expend some of his political capital in the inevitable battles with cabinet colleagues and American special interest groups. Certainly the residual National Security Affairs staff in the White House was in no position to undertake the complex, technical management of American relations with the enlarged European Community. In short, it would be done out of the State Department, or not at all.

A recurring suggestion is that an institutional link be established between the Community and the United States, as both Chancellor Brandt and Monnet's Action Committee for a United States of Europe had urged. The lack of mutual understanding and the multiple points of Atlantic friction supported the case for some formal political mechanism. In a disjointed European discussion of the subject in October 1972, Prime Minister Heath sided with Pompidou to quash Brandt's suggestion. Though British Foreign Office officials claimed that Heath's opposition was due to a conviction that a committee might exacerbate relations rather than improve them, it seems likely that his reservations rested on other considerations. Opposition to the joint committee was an issue on which Heath could align himself with Pompidou at low cost to British interests. And at that time Health still had confidence in his direct channel to Nixon.

During the Kennedy administration several *ad hoc* meetings were arranged between U. S. officials and President Hallstein and Vice-Presidents Marjolin and Mansholt of the Commission. Undersecretary of State George Ball chaired the American side, which included interested cabinet and sub-cabinet officials. With that precedent, a modest further step was taken in 1969 with the inauguration of semi-annual meetings of what came to be known as the Samuels-Dahrendorf Committee, so named for the United States' Deputy Undersecretary of State for Economic Affairs and the European Commissioner in charge of foreign affairs and trade policy. Although concrete results were modest, the committee was useful. It forced high-level attention, for at least a few moments, on the problems which bedeviled United States-Community relations. Because of the two principals' knowledge, interest, and good intentions, the periodic meetings encouraged American and Commission staffs to consider twice a year, in a reasonably orderly fashion, the full range of Atlantic economic problems. These meetings had a further benefit. The bureaucracies on both sides of the Atlantic lived in general ignorance of the broad context of American-Community relations, of the internal problems on the other side, and of their common interests. The sessions had the indirect value of bringing officials from domestic agencies together, under the aegis of the American half of the joint committee, renewing contacts between American and European opposite numbers in a larger setting.

The Samuels-Dahrendorf committee never received the formal sanction of the Council of Ministers, although the Commission periodically reported the results of the discussions to the Permanent Representatives or to the Council. The French dismissed the process as unnecessary, unworthy of serious attention, and extra-legal. The former French Permanent Representative questioned the authority which the Commission assumed in speaking without a Community mandate from the Council of Ministers. In fact, we fully recognized the importance of the other Community institutions and searched for some informal means of drawing the Permanent Representatives into the discussions which took place in Brussels. As a result, brief and highly informal meetings were held with members of the Committee of Permanent Representatives, but with no member of the Commission present. With the enlargement of the Community the joint committee was extended and somewhat strengthened. Soames, a Commission Vice-President, took over from Dahrendorf, and William Casey, with the elevated status of Undersecretary of State for Economic Affairs, replaced Samuels.

The constitutional questions advanced by the French were not entirely specious. The Commission is only one element of the complex Community structure. Effective consultation is impossible without some participation of the Council of Ministers and the Permanent Representatives. There is no easy way to accomplish this. One method would be to draw in either the President of the Council or the Chairman of the Committee of Permanent Representatives, who would then become spokesman for the nine. The negotiations for British entry and the

UNCTAD meeting in Santiago proved the stiff, lifeless quality of a procedure where the President of the Council of Ministers spoke for the Community. As an instructed agent he became a marionette whose strings were held by the member governments, constrained by negotiated instructions, and helpless when asked for explanation or expansion of his formal presentation. Dahrendorf rightly observed that the Council's participation would destroy informality without necessarily introducing responsibility. Yet if a joint committee is to be an effective device for communication, somehow or other the Council of Ministers must be involved. Thus the dilemma.

The American experience of joint cabinet committees with Canada and with Japan can hardly be called a spectacular success, and in the latter case must be judged a total failure in view of the tensions and misunderstandings across the Pacific. But the United States' problems with Japan and Canada did not arise out of governmental weakness, disorder, and confusion. The situation with the European Community is quite the contrary, for the Europeans have far to go before they have a government. A joint committee could be a means of drawing the Europeans together, ordering and elevating the discourse. For America, at least, it would intensify awareness that a Community exists, awareness of what it can and cannot do.

A New Cabinet-level Committee

The time has come to take advantage of America's and Europe's new concern about Atlantic relations, the enlargement of the Community, the rediscovery of the State Department, changes in American attitude, and the need to involve other Community institutions in the consultative process.

The political thrust of the Community and the need for a comprehensive American approach mean that only the Secretary of State can lead the American delegation. If the government ignores the United States' broad foreign policy interests in the Community, then the Secretary of the Treasury or the Assistant to the President for International Economic Affairs will arrogate responsibility for these relations, assuring that American-Community relations are handled in a purely economic context. The trend is in this direction. An informal committee co-chaired by an Undersecretary of State for Economic Affairs risks pre-emption.

As the Community evolves and creates problems within the interconnected world economy, Washington will be forced to pay closer attention. Inevitably, as cabinet officers become personally involved, the third ranking officer in the State Department lacks the status necessary to command a committee of cabinet secretaries. The strength of this bureaucratic pecking order asserted itself during the Department of State interregnum in mid-1974 following Casey's move to the Export-Import Bank. Leadership of the American delegation to one of the semi-annual U.S.-E.C. meetings slipped out of the hands of the Department and into those of the President's Special Representative for Trade.

The European side should be led by the President of the Commission, assisted by such commissioners as he determines, and the President of the Council of Ministers. While participation of the Council is essential, it would be ludicrous to envision a consultative committee which included nine foreign ministers in addition to the Commission representation. To deal with the requirement for member state attendance it would be possible, even desirable, to attach to the European delegation officials from the member governments, either from the capitals or from the Committee of Permanent Representatives.

Broadening the Committee to include the Council has limited advantages and real costs. It must be done, however, if the true dimension of the Community is to be accurately reflected. It is a part of the continuing educational process to enable American officials to confront the constitutional reality of the Community. There are even dangers in excessive emphasis on the Commission channel. As the United States interests itself in Community matters and the limited authority of the Commission becomes more evident, Washington might well overreact and attempt to do Community business through normal intergovernmental conduits. A joint cabinet-level committee with the Council participating would have the merit of keeping consultation within the Community system.

An advantage of the tested, informal U.S.-Commission mechanism has been its informality and the opportunity to discuss any economic issue. The addition of jurisdictionally-minded member state representatives to the committee, watchful of Commission pretensions and of possible invasions of national interests, would mean less interesting and, particularly for the Americans, more frustrating discussions. This cost, nonetheless, reflects the reality and the limits in constructing the Community.

Informality need not be a victim of a cabinet-level committee. Side discussions over luncheons have always been used to put back the substance lost in large, official meetings. One would expect the President of the Council, for example, in collateral conversations on the edges of a joint committee meeting, to become for a moment an informed foreign minister offering his candid personal views on Community business.

The semi-annual U.S.-E.C. meetings showed the need for greater care in developing the agenda, in preparing the sessions, and, at the conclusion, in insuring follow-up on the discussions. This experience should be applied to any more ambitious cabinet-level committee. One useful innovation which could be accomplished without excessive political pain would be to establish a joint secretariat. Much would be gained by holding an American and a European formally responsible for the effective functioning of the committee.

A further limitation on the committee technique is Washington. The open, complex joint-committee process is not a natural way of business for American administrations. An objective of the committee would be to nurse two big, diffused, inner-oriented bureaucracies into regular contact. One would hope that Washington could suppress its instinctive reservations about this obviously awkward device and see it as an indispensable means of assuring serious trans-Atlantic consultation.

For the foreseeable future a major problem will be how to deal with the Community's center of power, the member states. As the Council of Ministers, their agents, cannot be formally approached, the alternative is carefully planned contacts with the ministers in the capitals, especially with whichever foreign minister is sitting as president of the Council of Ministers. The American ambassadors to the nine countries, almost inevitably unfamiliar with Community business, are hardly the ideal instrument. They lack the knowledge essential to serious discussion with foreign ministers of substantive issues before the Community. Another technique, which was dramatized by Nixon–Kissinger diplomacy, is the special excursion or the direct intervention of the Secretary of State or other high Washington officials. This diplomatic weapon loses its edge quickly. Furthermore, the high visibility of the American Secretary's overt involvement in complex European affairs, and at what is likely to be an advanced stage of deliberation, can easily damage rather than advance the American case.

Kissinger's penchant and talent for personal diplomacy is matched by his suspicion of the bureaucracy. The Secretary's peripatetic mediation between Egypt and Israel produced awe, admiration, and unease. It was a brilliant, one-man show—with all the dangers implicit in that type of performance: as the supreme official he is denied the room for maneuver that is available to the normal negotiator who can disengage as he consults, or appears to consult, higher authority. Despite Kissinger's initial insistence that the State Department would be rebuilt and put back to work, it was personal, secretive diplomacy that persisted; his grip was so tight and the delegation of authority so minimal that it was impossible to get decisions on many urgent issues, including European policy. In examining the troubled state of the world and America's place in it, Alastair Buchan, in his 1973 Reith lectures, identified this problem. "By one of those ironies in which American history is so rich, Henry Kissinger, who in his writings has shared Metternich's contempt for bureaucracy but also lamented Bismarck's failure to create a government machine that could survive his own departure, may perceive that the best to which he can put his reputation and his remaining time in office will not be to reorganize the world, but to lay the foundations of reform that would give it greater confidence in the consistency of an American foreign policy less at the mercy of the vagaries of personality and political change. It would be as great a service to peace and world order as anything he could achieve by spinning round the world or by new concordats or démarches."[1]

Buchan's admonition applies exactly to future American relations with the member states and, more precisely, with the Council of Ministers. These relations will have to be supple, yet organized and institutionalized, not personalized. A variety of techniques will be involved. The American ambassador to the Community must have a larger mandate, one which will take him from time to time to the capitals to deal directly with ministers sitting on the various councils in Brussels. This will force some rethinking and readjustment of the role and of the traditional relationship for the American bilateral ambassadors to the host governments. In order to take full advantage of all of the resources available to the United States government, the professional staffs of the American embassies in the member countries must be fully and currently informed about the policies, problems, and structure of the Community, as well as of American policy.

1. *The Listener*, November 29, 1973, p. 743.

One of the most important channels to the member governments is through the Committee of Permanent Representatives, which has become the institutional *éminence grise* of the Community. Distrustful of the Commission and largely incapable of effective action itself, the Council of Ministers turns to the Permanent Representatives as its agent, as the possible means of finding that elusive compromise, even as a kind of alternative and controlled pseudo-Commission. The nine ambassadors (the Permanent Representatives) have thus been one of the most important contacts and sources of information for each of the foreign missions in Brussels, not least the U. S. Mission to the Community, but the nature of the Committee of Permanent Representatives and the extreme pressures on it preclude dealing with the Committee as a group.

As the Community evolves in its disorderly fashion, the American government will have to employ many devices if it is to maintain effective contact. For example, the expanding activities of the Community in the political field will pose special problems for Washington. The Political Committee floats from capital to capital, carrying its informal secretariat with it. The political sections of the American embassies do little more than catch up with these meetings after the fact. Anything other than post-mortem reporting will require that especially able American officers develop a rapport with several of the key political counselors among the nine (such as Davignon). If United States-Community relations can be brought to the point where informal exchanges of political information and planning become routine, then experts from Washington might meet periodically with the Political Committee.

A Web of Governmental and Private Contacts

Relations between the Community and the United States are far too serious to be left entirely to the mercy of governments. Though their central role cannot be ignored, means must be found to bring into continuous contact the various sectors of life in these pluralistic, democratic societies.

Future international relations will be largely an extension abroad of domestic activities. World monetary problems, for instance, are intensified when governments set domestic interest rates without reference to the international impact. The priority given to full employment policies has brought into question the effective operation of the trade and payments system. If domestic programs have these pervasive ramifications, a range of measures should be taken to sensitize interest groups to the far-reaching implications of what they might otherwise assume to be essentially national actions. One technique would be a long-term program, supported on both sides of the Atlantic, to develop a new network of close, professional contacts between Europeans and Americans. Limited steps in this direction have been taken with the Leader Grant Program run by USIA, and a similar program has been initiated by the Commission to reverse the process and bring Americans to Europe.

The Eisenhower Exchange Fellowships and the Commission have launched, on a trial basis, a new program for exchange visits of promising, middle-level, governmental experts in specific fields—such as energy, competition, and finance. The American expert assumes responsibility for arranging the program of his European counterpart for a month to six weeks in the United States, with the roles reversed when the American visits his European colleagues in Brussels. If the experiment succeeds, the technique should be expanded quickly. Extended and more intimate contacts between European and American experts, probing questions of public policy and profiting from a continuing exchange, could help revitalize Atlantic relations and correspond as well with the evolution of international relations in the direction of harmonizing domestic policies and programs. Strengthened academic exchanges can serve the same purpose. The lack of any American center for the study of the European Community, of even an academic clearing house, highlights our casual approach to contemporary European affairs.

Contacts between European and American business and industrial groups have grown rapidly. The International Chamber of Commerce, and other business organizations have been active. A different approach involves meetings between the European Group of Presidents, led by Comte René Boël on the European side and American business leaders. The Europeans especially have been interested in developing a systematic dialogue with company presidents or chairmen, engaging them in the entire range of common Community-United States interests, not merely in questions relating to immediate business concerns. The approach is novel, for it puts the executives in an active rather than passive role; they are not the traditional auditors at conferences run by the professional staffs of business organizations.

In contrast with other groups, relations between American and European labor have atrophied. The abrupt withdrawal of the AFL/CIO from the International Conference of Free Trade Unions cut another tie with Europe. The pretense was the hopelessly maladroit move by the then Secretary General of the ICFTU, Harm Buiter, to deal directly, even covertly, with Walter Reuther after the UAW had broken away from the AFL/CIO. The European interest in maintaining lines of communication with the UAW was understandable, given the compatibility of Reuther's view of the world, as contrasted with George Meany's, with that of European union leaders. But it was a clumsy exercise, the upshot of which was a near breakdown in formal relations between European and American labor, especially in regard to Community affairs.

A revival of relations perhaps could take the form of quiet, systematic meetings among American and European trade unionists around specific substantive issues of common concern. This procedure would accept the reality of AFL/CIO obduracy, avoiding further fruitless efforts to bring about a political settlement, and might lay a foundation for future reconciliation. The AFL/CIO's vigorous support of the Burke-Hartke bill and opposition to liberal trade proposals should be a warning of the damage which labor movements can do when they decide that their future interests—and jobs—rest on aggressive nationalism. A major effort should be made to reconstruct relations with European unions to avoid further estrangement of American and European labor.

Broader contacts among legislators should also be cultivated. As a separate and coequal branch of the government, the Congress is not prepared to become an adjunct of the executive branch in relations with the European Community. Senators and representatives may attend State Department luncheons and dinners and receive on the Hill distinguished Community visitors, but there has been no system to these random contacts. Former President Rey remained puzzled that, despite innumerable visits to Washington, he had never been able to meet Chairman Wilbur Mills of the Ways and Means Committee. As a result of patient instruction by the Delegation of the Community to the United States on the unique distribution of power within the American political system, visiting commissioners have come to appreciate the importance of informal meetings with senators and congressmen.

The riddle of Atlantic parliamentary relations arises from the functional committee structure of the Congress—Ways and Means, Finance,

Banking and Currency, Agriculture. The Foreign Affairs and Foreign Relations committees have responsibility for international affairs but lack authority on matters which are the bone and sinew of American relations with the Community. Atlantic parliamentary relations will be incomplete, even distorted, if the contacts between legislators rest exclusively within the province of the foreign policy groups, or, contrariwise, if the substantive committees pursue issues outside any political context.

The separate but equal governmental responsibility of the American Congress contrasts strikingly with the limited authority of most legislatures. Whatever the frustrations of the congressmen, they are officials with real political power and the envy of their European counterparts. Thus the obstacles to organizing an effective dialogue are formidable. The attention of overburdened American congressmen, absorbed with domestic matters and generally ill-informed about the Community, will be caught only by the dramatic issue. Yet the relationship between the United States and the Community demands real knowledge and a degree of mutual understanding among the legislators.

A start has been made. Led by Ben Rosenthal, while Chairman of the European Subcommittee of the House Foreign Affairs Committee, a regular, semi-annual exchange with the members of the European Parliament was established. The meetings have not been restricted to members of the Foreign Affairs Committee; congressmen expert in other fields have been included. For this kind of relationship to flourish, ingenuity, informality, and flexibility are required. The normal workings of the Congress and of the member states' parliaments, the oppressive weight of familiar procedures, committees and seniority, and, on the European side, the balancing of national and political party representation must be surmounted. Rather than the thin generality of the customary interparliamentary conclave, the House-European Parliament meetings have involved intensive joint studies of specific subjects like agriculture, foreign aid, and energy, based on papers prepared by individual legislators. In contrast with the initiative and interest shown by the House, the Senate has maintained intact its indifference to and ignorance of the European Community, although individual senators have made their way to the Community—Senators Javits, Ribicoff, Mathias, Mondale, and a few others. The Senate Foreign Relations Committee has ignored the Community, as it has forgotten Western Europe. When asked whether something should not be done to draw the attention of that committee to the enlarged European Community, one of its senior staff members advised, "Leave well enough alone."

This is an area where nongovernmental European and American organizations can help. They have flexibility, and on a given subject they can invite from the various parliamentary bodies the most informed and responsible legislators. Through this method small groups can be gathered together, for example, at Ditchley Park or Arden House for intensive discussions. A relationship based on systematic, informed inquiry into matters within the special competence of the participants could lay the foundation for future, more formal arrangements between the Congress and European parliamentarians.

A broad spectrum of nongovernmental activity would pay rich dividends; generating understanding could insure that the convulsive reactions of governments to economic or political crises do not swamp Atlantic relations. The disinterested nature of these contacts, the fact that they grow out of renewed American interest in Western Europe, could redress in part the sour image of America fixed in the European mind. Immediately after Nixon's resignation the British Gallup Poll discovered that only three in ten of the British had any special confidence in America's ability to cope with world problems. Too many Europeans, particularly the youth, have come to accept what one hopes is a caricature of the United States—ruthless bombing of small countries, covert activities against governments it does not like, urban blight and violence at home, corrupt and powerless government. This image might be improved by the imaginative efforts of the people on both sides, recapturing some of the creative spirit of earlier days, seeking to re-identify the common interests of Europe and America.

European and American Policy Imperatives

On the substantive side, Washington's lack of interest in the Community's efforts to develop European foreign policies based on consensus has been absolute. For years the Department of State's European Bureau largely ignored the subject. When this was no longer possible, it assigned the backstopping of the Davignon Committee in the Department to officers responsible for NATO. Intradepartmental coordination was uninspiring—but in its own way instructive. Admittedly it is a complicated problem in organization. The nascent European political activity is carried on outside the formal European Community system; furthermore the subject matter falls in the general domain of foreign policy and bears different bureaucratic labels—Middle East, Eastern Europe, and so forth. For the Department to be effective, the competence of the various political experts must be brought to bear on the subjects being considered by the Europeans. Washington's principal reaction to the first excursion of the Europeans into political issues was some handwringing, a worry that they were developing a clique which would upset traditional bilateral relations or harm the club spirit of the NATO Council.

Earlier, note was made of the Community's intrinsic problems to be met in developing and executing foreign policy. The experience with the Declaration of Principles and the internal tangles among the Europeans over Middle East policy reveal another basic problem: the breadth of disagreement among the nine as to what Community policy should be. The British and the Danes would be content with no foreign policy at all. The Irish, with the departure of Prime Minister Lynch, withdrew a suggestion that Ireland would be prepared to play a part in Western defense. Giscard seemed less a captive than were de Gaulle and Pompidou to the Gallic assertion that France's natural bent lay in diplomacy. Nonetheless, given the tradition of Talleyrand and the undeniable competence of the French civil servant, it would be prudent to assume that Paris would continue to urge on its colleagues French foreign policy prescriptions as the best bases for a Community foreign policy.

In contrast to the difficulty of foreign policy as a subject for the Community, economics involves generally measurable phenomena which suggest somewhat measurable alternative responses. An agricultural problem, for example, has objective characteristics, and remedial courses of action emerge. But the question of whether and under what conditions Spain might become a member of the European Community is painfully subjective. Paris has favored Spanish membership for economic and security reasons related to French interests. French officials have been unperturbed by the absence of Spanish democratic instincts or institutions. Others in the Community have not shared the trade and defense preoccupations the French, but have been acutely conscious of Spain's democratic deficiencies.

For the nation-state, the foreign policy decision-making process comes down finally to a personal judgment by one man—a president, prime minister, or foreign minister. The man, is, of course, hedged in by domestic pressures, colleagues, and political constraints, but the decision is his. The Community's lack of an effective decision-making process, which slows economic union, will confound even more the construction of Community foreign policy. Political subjects which are highly sub-jective drift helplessly within a system where the most important ele-ment is unanimity. It is a superb formula for the production of foreign policy homilies.

Basic to this complex subject is American attitude. There have been spasmodic changes. For years, among the few who cared, the attitude was despair as the eternal European discussion went on in search of the elusive Community consensus. The long period of general indiffer-ence to Europe's unsuccessful efforts was forgotten in Kissinger's scolding of their pretensions in attempting to define a Middle East policy in the fall of 1973. The excessive umbrage with which Jobert and the Quai d'Orsay responded to the Secretary's provocation, although deplored publicly in other capitals, in fact reflected a general, if sup-pressed European irritation at Washington's deportment. One did not need to be a Frenchman to resent the implication that Washington had a right to insert itself openly into intra-European deliberations, and at the most preliminary stages. With equal suddenness a few months later, Kissinger declared that harmony and good will had been restored. Al-though relieved that open sniping had ceased, Europeans had few il-lusions and concluded that, at best, Washington had decided to tolerate their common foreign policy efforts, but underneath persisted in its dislike of the idea.

With the internal hurdles so substantial it is hard to see how the Community can hope to succeed if Washington's attitude is unsympa-thetic. Indeed, in addition to sincere, not merely verbal, support there should be particular sensitivity to the implication for the Community of foreign policy issues, and an effort to counterbalance that inevitable bias towards exclusively bilateral channels. Furthermore, the relation-ship of desk officer to desk officer and the ambiance of the club of foreign secretaries produce an almost irresistible, gravitational force toward the traditional diplomatic channels.

Washington will not find it easy to adjust to the new, two-pillar Atlantic world. Even to those Americans not given to dreams of dominance, it would be an unsettling change from the comfortable pattern of the NATO Political Committee. The temptation, and opportunities, would be to insinuate the United States into the internal Community process. And there would be Europeans who see their interests served by American involvement; it would be hard to resist drawing in a powerful ally if it might strengthen one's own case in the European debate. Furthermore, some foreign office officials, and by no means merely the Anglo-Saxons, frequently feel more comfortable with American colleagues, whether in the European capitals or in Washington, than they do with their European associates.

There are several obvious political subjects for American-European discussion. The oil crisis made the Middle East both a key yet an impossible topic. Deep disagreements among the Europeans were combined with differences between Europe and the United States. America's political commitment to Israel and more limited dependence on imported energy were fundamentally incongruent with European perceptions and interests. Had there been mutual confidence between the two sides of the Atlantic, the crisis would still have imposed severe strains. And as there had been no joint examination of the problems with their political, economic, and security implications before the October 1973 explosion, it was hard to initiate any orderly, staff-level exploration in the midst of the wreckage. Nor was this prospect helped by the outbreak of war on Cyprus. Europe's impotence was again on public display —Britain the guarantor of Cypriot independence, unable to prevent its *de facto* partition; Germany without influence despite its traditional ties to Turkey; the Community's association arrangements with Greece and Turkey useless; and finally, NATO not merely ignored, but perhaps permanently weakened. It stretches the imagination to believe that the most effectively organized Community, collaborating with the United States in perfect accord, could have averted the crisis. Nonetheless, continuing, intensive American-Community political discussions of the many facets of the Middle East and Mediterranean could at least have developed a framework within which these and subsequent problems might have been handled.

Greece, Turkey, then Portugal, and later perhaps Spain, each seems beyond the effective reach of NATO, or the bilateral diplomacy of the United States or the major European countries. Although disorganized, dissonant, and politically undeveloped, the Community nonetheless has one great source of potential strength: its economic weight. Is there no way this asset—vast market, capital, skills, demand for foreign labor—can be employed in this critical region? In addition to the overriding importance of the Community to these Mediterranean countries, its unique advantage is that it does not carry the heavy political weight of the old European nations.

East-West relations, as they become increasingly complicated, should be a permanent topic of conversation. A systematic, candid dialogue can ease some of the tensions and suspicions of American policy that may otherwise become intolerable. Political discourse of this sort may minimize the risks of misunderstandings growing out of the separate games being played in various places—MBFR in Vienna, SALT II and the Conference on European Security in Geneva, intermittent conversations in Moscow and in the course of the ceaseless travels of foreign ministers.

Kissinger's emphasis on United States-Soviet relations during the Nixon era makes it especially important that Washington avoid any hint of associating itself with Soviet policies toward the Community. It is insufficient that Washington may have a clear conscience; its comportment should dispel even unreasonable doubts. Part of the answer is complete candor, a steady flow of information about the United States-Soviet dialogue to the member states and, on economic matters, to the Commission. The only beneficiary of secrecy is the U.S.S.R.

American interests would be served by a common Community policy toward the East. Step by painful step Europe moves in this direction. The evolution has become easier as experience has led the Community members to discard expectation of extravagant economic gain from bilateral relations with Eastern Europe. To the extent that the Western Europeans work together, it becomes more difficult for the Russians to play one country off against another or, conversely, for the competitive instinct to take over with each Western European country seeking to improve its position with the East against its Community partners. With a common position the Community, working with the United States, could have a moderating influence on the Soviet Union. Subsiding Western European hopes for economic and political miracles have coincided with the thawing of American policy toward the Soviet Union, making conditions ripe for Atlantic cooperation.

It would be logical for Europeans to stress, in the pursuit of unity, those fields where the Rome Treaty is clear and extension into related foreign policy is almost unavoidable. Community development along these economic-political lines would correspond with the growing international attention being given to economic factors. It would have the further advantage of drawing on the staff competence of the existing Community. Indeed, events may be sufficiently powerful to propel Europe forward in spite of itself. If the political impetus finds its strength in economic interests and problems, then the Community is in tune with the future. A slow convergence of economic and political factors could limit the tendency of the existing European Community to march off in one direction while European political union attempts a different course with separate institutions and people. Europe would suffer a severe blow if the Community under the Treaty of Rome should be restricted to purely economic activities, with political matters handled as entirely discrete phenomena. This would ignore the present structure of Europe and the gathering force of economic factors. The energy crisis was to be Europe's crucial test, for its all-encompassing nature ruled out the artificial division between politics and economics, as it exposed the impossibility of purely national solutions.

Although America cannot anticipate the process of European political unification, it would be folly to stand rooted in the past, to move only in response to some absolutely clear and unanimous signal. Washington should be closely attuned to the direction of European movement, judge its strength, and then devise American actions to assist the process. Any problem or crisis requires an estimate of the European interests at stake and a judgment as to how the United States and the nine can deal with it together. In the future the reflex telephone call to Downing Street or the Elysée can be no more than a part of a more complex American-Community collaboration, with new habits easy for neither side.

Chapter VIII

The Community and Defense

Of the three major substantive areas—economics, politics and defense—the latter has moved glacially, if at all. The inherent difficulties of the subject, memories of past failures—the ill-fated European Defense Community, the Multilateral Nuclear Force, French withdrawal from the integrated military command of NATO—hang over the Europeans. The sheer magnitude of the problems, the divergence of national interests, and the preoccupation with other Community issues have encouraged Europe to temporize. Many of the difficulties have been of European making, but America has contributed to them.

Almost absent-mindedly, the Johnson administration struck two hard blows at nascent European defense unification, with collateral shocks to European unification and American-European relations. After extensive efforts by his administration to promote the Multilateral Nuclear Force (MLF), with limited but significant European support, suddenly in 1965 President Johnson decided to capsize it. The MLF had been conceived in order to bring together under the aegis of a joint project those Western European nations which wished to participate in an Atlantic nuclear weapons system. It was an imaginative effort to associate the non-nuclear allies, such as Italy, the Netherlands, and especially Germany, with the military nuclear powers in a common endeavor which might have formed the basis for a future European defense union. Furthermore, the project involved new organic links between the Europeans and the United States. From its inception, the MLF was controversial on both sides of the Atlantic.

Without raking over the arguments, pro and con, the narrow point to be made is that the manner in which America dropped a project, which it had initiated and vigorously led, caused lasting damage among the Europeans. A number of leading German, British, Dutch, and Italian political figures, each committed to European unity and, coincidentally, to close ties with the United States, had endorsed the MLF and had invested in it personal prestige. Such men as Gerhard Schröder, then German Foreign Minister, were injured by Johnson's impetuous action. That Washington would take such a step without consultation was sobering. In the future, European leaders would be careful before mooring their political fortunes to unpredictable and possibly cavalier American leadership.

The second blow to European aspirations was the concession made by the American government to the Russians in the negotiation of the treaty on the Non-Proliferation of Nuclear Weapons (NPT). From the point of view of many Europeans the treaty was a curious diplomatic exercise; it was an arms control measure worked out by the two major nuclear powers, but it involved no limitations on their own arms, no sacrifice of their own immediate interests. America's contribution was to insure that its non-nuclear allies would remain non-nuclear. Pressure on the Europeans to accept this imposed self-denial left scars and ill will.

As is so often the case, Washington was trying to reconcile several policy objectives. The arms control aspect of the NPT was obvious. But there was also the American interest in leaving the way open to further European integration, especially in the field of defense. Without willing or even predicting the ultimate outcome, the argument was made that the treaty should not preclude some eventual combination of the British and the French military nuclear forces; furthermore, if the Europeans decided that the merged force would be the core of a European military program, then the treaty should permit rather than obstruct this evolution. The logic was clear; the treaty's objective was to prevent the emergence of additional military nuclear powers; a merger of two existing national forces and development of a European nuclear entity would not increase the number of military nuclear states.

Europeans close to the development of the Community could envision a model. The need to rationalize the nuclear programs of the French and British would coincide with growing European interest in a common defense effort which would, in turn, generate a momentum leading to both political and defense unity and, eventually, to a European state. This possible European nuclear evolution could have been the cutting edge for further, general European unity, not merely a hypothetical end result. The United States seemed to agree, but when the Russians proved unyielding in their opposition to this concept, the American negotiators finally retreated and accepted provisions which ruled out the evolutionary process. In his interpretative comments to the Senate on the treaty, Secretary Rusk insisted that the NPT did not preclude a "European political state" from inheriting the assets of its constituent members. But this American interpretation meant that a full-fledged federal European union would have to come into being first, as a condition to the transfer of the French and British military nuclear programs to any European entity. In light of the manner in which the European Community has evolved, the "solution" Rusk outlined seems totally illusory.

There has been no European groundswell for a defense union. The large and the small countries face in opposite directions, the former conscious of defense requirements, the latter drawn by détente and caught in the current of pacifist political forces at home. And the larger countries see things by no means the same way. France began to make ambiguous noises about European defense when Foreign Minister Jobert referred in vague terms to a new future for the moribund Western European Union. But the hard substance of French policy was still rooted in independence and fidelity to Gaullist dogma. Consistent with the General's principles, France remained outside the NATO Eurogroup, while insisting that any return of France to the military side of NATO was unthinkable. Germany's overriding defense interest has been to protect the integrity of the American commitment in Europe, to do nothing which might in any way shake that commitment or encourage the withdrawal of American forces. Certainly, the Russians and the Eastern Europeans could be relied on to use *Ostpolitik* as a whiplash against the Germans should they begin to show an active interest in including defense in European union.

The smaller countries have traditionally viewed such ideas with reserve. The Dutch gave some support to the MLF, but, in general, their defense policy is anchored to the Atlantic system. The Danes, Belgians, and Norwegians have been cool to any European defense connection, indeed to defense costs in general; they have contented themselves with arrangements which left the principal burden on the shoulders of their allies. Allied defense efforts are in the retractive phase, moving slowly in some countries, rapidly in others. But there is no question about the direction.

Whatever the difficulties in the way of economic or political union, they pale in comparison with those in the defense field. Defense is the ultimate expression of national sovereignty; it is the quintessence of the unholy marriage between industry and government—that network of ties between legislatures, business, and defense establishments. The obvious absurdity of small nations maintaining supposedly balanced defense forces in the day of $100 million destroyers stimulates no urgent search for alternative, more rational arrangements. Despite more than two decades' experience with NATO, despite the assignment to it of certain headquarters functions, and despite cooperation in several joint production programs, the alliance is still only an association of independent, national states. Can it be different in the Community?

Defense and nationhood are so intertwined that even limited transfer of military functions to some new supranational body seems almost visionary. Defense poses, in ultimate form, the question: Who decides? Who sends the forces to war? The open, fumbling Community system with its commitment to unanimity scarcely works in the economic area. Its most ardent supporter could not imagine this Europe effectively managing modern arms and coping with a military crisis.

Pressures and Possibilities for European Collaboration

Despite these difficulties, there is a kind of inevitability that Europe, over time, will be driven to form a defense union. Indeed, if it does not unify its military efforts, the Community, like the Cheshire cat, will slowly fade until only the smile is left. As an objective, European defense union deserves strong American support.

One thing is certain; NATO in its classical form, with its manpower and military resources, will not continue unchanged. Pressures come from every side. Détente is an unpredictable force for change, which many will use as an excuse to reduce defense expenditures. Some feel that negotiations to limit arms necessitate a strong defense posture as an essential bargaining chip; to others, negotiations offer the opportunity to cut military costs at once. America's debates over defense policy and the budget are bellwethers for the alliance. Despite the Nixon administration's effective holding action, Congressional opponents continue their assault on the Seventh Army in Germany. Buffeted by the economic un-certainties of 1974, could the Ford administration win continuing victories against the Mansfield forces? The Gallup poll in October 1973 showed about 60 percent of the public favoring a reduction of American forces abroad, almost the same percentage as those who believed defense expenditures were too high. As a general rule, minds which have begun to close on the notion of NATO's relevance are not likely to assess objectively the West's security problems, or propose new arrangements to meet them.

On both sides of the Atlantic the general public reaction to the Western defense problem is to evade the issue in the hope that some combination of devices will buy time. Unquestionably, the underlying situation has radically altered: a markedly different political and military East-West relationship, an affluent and partially unified Western Europe, and a dif-ferent United States. Multiple arms control negotiations, the possible or probable withdrawal of some American forces, and an enlarged Euro-pean Community should stir Europe to examine the security issue in a new dimension and to explore the means of assuming greater responsi-bility for Western defense. The only chance for a substantial European military contribution, even for a continuation of defense budgets at 1973–1974 levels, lies in some form of common European defense action.

Certain obstacles to consideration of the European security issue have been removed. The British had first to finish their negotiations to become members of the Community; the Germans, to extract from *Ostpolitik* the arrangements with East Germany and the Berlin Treaty; the French, to conclude the 1974 elections and then limit the influence of the ultra-Gaullists. Although the smaller countries pose a serious problem, they too seemed ready for new discussions. The process can be helped along by expressions of Washington's support for European defense unity; some Europeans doubt that that sympathy exists. Certainly, America should avoid adding hurdles to the formidable array already in place.

Perhaps in the new European atmosphere, proposals will emerge from academic and nongovernmental groups. They are unlikely to come from the national defense establishments or from NATO. The human re-sources exist, for instance, in the International Institute for Strategic Studies, in the Atlantic Institute, and in numerous American and Euro-pean academic centers—and these experts may be able to fill the present vacuum.

There are four logical areas for exploration. The first would be a rationalization of European forces in being and committed to NATO. Without major political or defense upheaval, the European member states with forces in Germany could consider a range of actions designed to conserve resources, simplify common structures, and enhance the effectiveness of present forces. The second area is Community production of military items in common use. The member states spend approximately $22 billion each year on defense. The efficient use of this money would mean the procurement of better products at less cost and bring the benefits of standardization, at the same time freeing resources for other urgent defense needs.

Dutch plans to reduce military expenditures illustrate the dangers, and the possibilities. When asked if this policy was not due to weariness with defense, the State Secretary of the Dutch Defense Ministry replied, "Not yet. We wanted to shock NATO. . . . Our purpose is to bring about more standardized armament of the troops of all NATO partners. If the great powers—America, Britain, France and Germany—agree on one tank system, one or two anti-tank systems, two aircraft types, then also the small countries will be able to hold their own. If standardization is not achieved soon, the Netherlands will no longer play its part." The State Secretary went on to say that there would be no standardization if the major countries continued to consider exclusively their own armament industries. But if progress could be made in general standardization, then the Dutch, for example, would be prepared to affiliate their air force with the *Bundeswehr*. High maintenance costs make it increasingly impractical for small countries to support national air forces. The threat was clear. For when it was suggested that he seemed to envision withdrawal from NATO, the State Secretary said, "Not quite. Politically we will stay on. But militarily we would get out in 1979."[1]

The third area is that of sophisticated weapons and the relationship of their production to Europe's interest in encouraging advanced technology. There is a natural interconnection between the Community's industrial ambitions and defense production. A move in this direction would pose a hard dilemma for the United States. On the one hand, more unified and effective European defense would contribute directly

1. Interview with State Secretary Stemerdink in *Bild*, cited in *Daily Press Review*, USIS, American Embassy, Bonn, July 12, 1974.

to American security. On the other, European defense unification would adversely affect American economic interests. Sales of sophisticated weapons to Europe not only support American arms manufacture, already plagued by declining domestic orders, but are of importance to America's external accounts. It would be wise, however, to read the handwriting on the wall and recognize that inevitably Europe will meet many of its requirements for sophisticated weapons out of its own production. At least the impact will be felt only over an extended period of time, for the development of European production is a long-term process.

The fourth area is nuclear weapons: the prospective collaboration or even merger of the British and the French military nuclear programs. The variations on this theme run from technological exchange and production to the actual consolidation of the nuclear forces. Over the years Anglo-French nuclear cooperation has been a favorite military parlor game. A gambit would be offered by one side or the other, then withdrawn. At one stage Heath alluded to such collaboration with France, as had French defense experts. Wilson's chauvinism, however, and Giscard's sufficient agenda of contentious issues with the Gaullists, to say nothing of the frosty relations between the two governments, were quite enough to relegate this idea to the bottom of pending issues. Should the matter be revived at some stage in the future, it is not a question America can evade.

The British nuclear weapon program draws heavily on American technology. The United States' acquiescence (specifically that of the Joint Committee on Atomic Energy of the Congress) would be required before the British could cooperate fully with the French. A decision to do so, in the absence of American consent, would lead automatically to a cutoff of access to American technology in view of the consistent distaste of the Congress for sharing nuclear information with the French. If, despite these problems, the French and the British should decide to embark on a policy of nuclear collaboration and the sharing of military technology, one would expect the effects on the general East-West arms control negotiations to be adverse.

There are other major issues. Would a merger be a conscious way station to some new European defense community; or would it, by intent or by eventual corruption of the process, be merely a device for Franco-British hegemony over their non-nuclear European allies? Further, there seems to be no way in which the combined French and British forces and production could replace American tactical and strategic weapons and delivery systems, which are now a major element in European defense.

One of the most intractable problems, one which has consistently confounded American and European policy-makers, is Germany and nuclear weapons. The Western European Union Treaty, the Non-Proliferation Treaty, the attitudes of allies and enemies, and of the Germans themselves, rule against an independent German nuclear force. Yet Germany is at the center of Western defenses, presumably a principal Soviet target. If there is to be a Western security system, German manpower, money, territory, and political commitment must be integrally tied to the resources of its partners in the Community and in NATO. A merger of French and British nuclear forces would highlight the disparity between the nuclear and non-nuclear powers at a time when these weapons have taken on increasing importance and when the likely reduction of American conventional forces would imply less credibility to the American nuclear guaranty. The upshot of a French-British merger would be intensification of German unease and a sense of discrimination.

It is a problem which defies solution. The most dangerous course would be to assume that, no matter what France and Britain should decide to do, the Germans would remain docile and content. The older Germans, whose memories of World War II remain fresh, accepted discrimination; it would be risky to assume that the new generation will follow patiently in their parents' footsteps. It would be an historic tragedy if the benefits of European unification, especially the organic association of the Federal Republic with its neighbors within the framework of the European Community, were to be negated by mishandling the nuclear component.

If the problem cannot be solved by creating either an Anglo-French or a European nuclear force, then it must be managed somehow. And in fact it has been managed; the circle remains squared, due to the delicate compromise and the sensitive allied appreciation of the explosive nature of the nuclear dilemma. By drawing Germany into planning, nuclear targeting, strategy, indeed everything short of weapon ownership and weapon control, the line within the alliance which distinguishes the nuclear from the non-nuclear countries has been carefully obscured. The arrangement has been made to work because each of the parties knows it must, and recognizes the price that would have to be paid should it collapse.

When casting about for incentives for European unity, it is tempting to consider experimentation with shock therapy. Pessimistic about the ability of any administration to hold off forever pressure to reduce the American NATO forces, some observers wonder if the drama of this action might not force Europe to do more than temporize. No solid case can be made for shock therapy in politics. The defeat of the European Defense Community in 1954 did prepare the ground for the Messina conference and the Euratom and the Economic Community treaties. But the veto of British entry and de Gaulle's further actions against his partners drove them not to more ambitious enterprises, but to husband their strength. Similarly, the energy and the financial crises sent them reeling rather than on to basic inquiry of what Europe could do together.

It is beyond the scope of this book to argue the brief for maintaining substantial American forces in Europe on grounds of American interest: that this commitment is essential to America's own defense; that withdrawal across the Atlantic would not help the American defense budget; and that it would be the signal for which the Soviet Union has long waited. It is relevant, however, to weigh carefully the adverse effects of such a step on European cohesion and on American-European relations. If the United States were to cut back substantially its forces, precipitously and without attention to the impact on Europe, the results would unquestionably be conducive to the spread of the kind of blind neutralism and nationalism demonstrated by the New Progress party in Denmark. A sudden blow of this sort would confront Europe with another dilemma, insoluble certainly in the near term. Decisions to strengthen the common defense would not be the likely outcome. Acceptable Atlantic relations must avoid, if at all possible, that kind of crisis.

In attempting to pierce the murky future and speculate about lines of European movement on defense matters, one glimpses possibilities rather than probabilities. Limited intellectual effort has been devoted to the subject; a European consensus has not even begun to appear. An almost insurmountable problem has been Gaullist policy and attitude. It is hard to see how a start can be made as long as one of the key participants throws up dogmatic obstacles of inviolate national independence, is obstinately unwilling to collaborate with the NATO Eurogroup, remains outside the NATO Nuclear Planning Group, and attaches its divisions in Germany only tenuously to other allied forces.

The obvious instrument at hand for European exploration is the Eurogroup. Initiated by the British in 1968, it includes ten of the European members of NATO (all but France and Ireland among the Community members). It has encouraged consultation among the Europeans in advance of discussion within the NATO Council, launched studies related to cost-effectiveness and closer cooperation by the Europeans, and made a substantial contribution to the problem of burden-sharing through the European Defense Improvement Program.

The next step beyond the Eurogroup might be the establishment of a defense committee of the nine, patterned on the Davignon Committee. Composed of senior defense experts from the governments, with an independent secretariat, the committee could have as its primary mission the rationalizing of the Community resources presently devoted to defense. The defense committee would report to a council of defense ministers. From this familiar structure, a defense organization could develop parallel to that of the Council of Ministers and the European Commission in the economic field. Close cooperation between the two areas would be essential in view of the interrelationship of defense budgets, weapons research, development and production, and the Community's range of economic responsibilities, with coordination at the ministerial level. An organizational arrangement of this sort would not be institutionally innovative, but it could initiate the process of unifying European defense efforts.

Europe has three, broad, fundamental policy choices: (1) acceptance of the present situation, drifting along and hoping for the best; (2) concentration on a nuclear strategy and on nuclear weapons; or (3) a European effort centered on conventional forces, the weapons to support these forces, the rationalization of national defense programs, and the effective deployment and logistical and administrative support of this conventional defense system. The first option would be an admission of impotence and failure. There is not, in fact, a nuclear option. In the absence of a tenable alternative, concentration on conventional weapons and forces is therefore the only course open to Europe.

The Need for an American Policy

An effective Western defense requires a seamless web of conventional and nuclear forces and weapons, of combined American and European resources, and of the mutual commitment of both sides of the Atlantic relationship. The insoluble nuclear problem and the inescapable European dependence on American nuclear weapons and the American guaranty create a critical psychological problem. America has to sense the dimensions and the sensitivity of this problem and deal with it so that the essence of the Atlantic relationship is intimate cooperation, not American superiority and European subordination. Cooperation presupposes a reinforcing process of American policy aiding the growth of Europe's self-confidence which will develop in measure with its political and economic union. In this climate, determined European separateness in the military field would be less compelling. European defense would assume the improbability of the use of nuclear weapons; Western security would be concentrated on conventional defense. A further assumption is that the United States would share its advanced non-nuclear technology with Europe and accept the fact that substantial production would be performed there.

As European defense collaboration progressed, there would be the possibility of restructuring NATO into a new arrangement, under the general umbrella of the Treaty, with a military structure composed of two major pillars, America and a united Europe. Such a solution could open the way for French participation, since it would not be vulnerable to attack as blasphemy of General de Gaulle's sacred precepts. Within the framework of a tighter Atlantic defense community, the distinction between nuclear and non-nuclear power would diminish.

In sum, America should impress upon its European allies that it sympathizes with the efforts they might wish to take to unify European defense; that there are no latent American reservations; that, rather than precipitate American withdrawal, European initiatives in the defense area could be essential in insuring continued participation by the United States in the common defense.

Chapter IX

Epilogue

As the end of my years in Brussels approached, I welcomed escape from the government and the opportunity to reflect, away from official pressures and responsibilities, on the future course of American-European relations. Reducing these reflections to written form seemed then a simple task: describe the objective situation, the current state of the Community, the economic and political setting, and American attitudes and policy; and, with this in hand, let the prescription emerge.

Some reference to my dashed expectations is in order. All the reader need do is compare the end of 1972 with the end of 1974, just two years. January 1973 seemed an authentic turning point for Europe, from stalemate to fresh movement. With the settlement of the British question, at issue for twenty years, and enlargement of the Community accomplished, one could reasonably believe that French policy was evolving from the obstructionism of Gaullism. While inflation was worrisome, nonetheless, the European economy boomed, even holding the promise of lifting Britain out of its perennial doldrums. Nixon's 1972 electoral triumph implied, among other things, continued priority to foreign policy, with new emphasis on Europe, even though American diplomacy could be expected to employ the tested Nixon-Kissinger instruments—secrecy, confrontation, surprise—within an adversary environment.

Whatever else the events of 1973 and 1974 proved, they underscored the hazard of prophecy. Orderly evolution dissolved into climactic change, unanticipated, indigestible. Inflation and economic crises undermined the expectation of continued growth. Europe could no longer expect that a steadily expanding economy would ease the way toward unity by floating the Community over the many barriers in its way.

The political upheaval was awesome. Nixon's dizzy course, from victory to White House siege to resignation, was consistent with political change everywhere. Britain turned from earnest new member into neo-Gaullist, obstructive, threatening withdrawal. Europeans seriously wondered whether the social fabric of Britain could survive inflation, stagnation, and incipient class warfare, or whether Italy could avoid bankruptcy. In Germany and France a new generation of technocrat-pragmatists who would profoundly influence European politics had come to power.

As one sat in the midst of the broken crockery, the nagging question was whether there was any pattern behind it all. There was still the ill-defined support for European unity, even in the United Kingdom as the obscure battle between the Trades Union Congress and the moderates of the Parliamentary Labour Party drifted from London to Brighton. The resurrection of Franco-German intimacy recalled the original motor of European progress.

The abrupt departure of so many political leaders brought into question Kissinger's proclivity for resting international affairs exclusively on personal relations among heads-of-government. For those of us who thought the cycle of European crises and stalemate was broken, we could only recant and accept the fact that there would always be European problems. Gaullism was still alive and well in Brussels, only the language of obstruction was now English. Agriculture proved that it could be unmanageable under any set of economic conditions.

The search for the continuing threads revealed the strength of nationalism, in both America and Europe, the related obsession with domestic matters, and the complementary emergence of, not isolationism, but new forms of anti-internationalism. A strong thread was the unremitting European struggle to escape oppressive American domination. Manifestly impossible in defense or in superpower politics, and disconcertingly more distant in economics, the compulsive drive for a degree of independence sought outlet in other areas and other ways.

Despite all the turmoil, disputes, and misunderstandings, one basic constant has remained in the minds of responsible Americans and Europeans: the common interest in preserving the Atlantic relationship. As the agenda of problems lengthened—inflation, energy deficits, threats to the international financial system, food shortages, world population explosion—European and Americans accepted, however grudgingly, that there was no chance whatever of solutions without American-European collaboration.

In this connection one wonders whether the Nixon-Kissinger diplomacy will turn out to have been aberrant or will be the enduring new form of American foreign policy. In terms of strategy, tactics, and style, it had been a relationship of perfect harmony between President and Secretary of State. In certain ways this diplomatic practice all too accurately reflected the domestic mood—the desire to limit commitments, the instinct for adversary relations and the excitement that the use, and abuse, of power creates. The encouragement of these anti-internationalist tendencies hardly eased the task of those who must administer American foreign policy in the future. There are other legacies. The soft background music of Atlantic harmony and devotion to Europe cannot block out the public memories of years of errors and omissions, interrupted by sharp charges and angry responses. A price must be paid for the degradation of language, of words emptied of meaning. A costly legacy may be the degree to which the Nixon-Kissinger diplomacy transposed the American public from participant to spectator—invited to observe, but not expected to become involved.

When applied to American-Community relations some elements of this inherited diplomacy may turn out to be durable. The skepticism of large ideas and of institutions may reinforce popular doubts about the end results, or even the possibility, of European unity. A pessimistic American public is certainly prone to expect the worst from its allies and to cast European actions in the least favorable light. While this mood prevails, Kissinger's exercise of power toward Europe is more congenial to the public than would be the exercise of restraint, or of forbearance. Fatigued by foreign affairs and roused only by crises, the American public plays neatly into the scenario of recent diplomacy.

The initial moves of the Ford administration were entirely consistent with this style. Giscard d'Estaing, in the course of his first television speech in August 1974 to his countrymen, which dealt principally with domestic affairs, alluded to the political change in the United States, ". . . during this changeover the outgoing president and the incoming president gave speeches on domestic and foreign affairs and in neither of these two speeches was the word Europe spoken." Then, after touching on the problem flowing from Cyprus, he drew two conclusions; the first, ". . . that Europe must only count on itself to organize and the second is that the modern world will not truly be the modern world until the map ceases to be torn where Europe should be." Rather than ignoring Giscard's moderately provocative statement or turning it to advantage, Kissinger directed a snap White House comment: ". . . the record of commitment to our alliance and to Europe is clear. The President (Ford) looks forward to a productive and cooperative relationship with France and other friends in Europe as well as with the existing and emerging institutions of the European Community." It was vintage Kissinger—implicit rejection of the charge, insistence that all is well, the bandaid of reiterated policy, and the promise of early high-level exchanges. It was not an encouraging omen.

It is difficult to be optimistic about any early change in style or policy content, and not merely because of Kissinger's monopoly of American foreign policy. Crisis diplomacy, personally manipulated, unfortunately corresponds to the instincts of the European pragmatists and the universal surge of nationalism. It will not be easy to lay aside egocentric diplomacy and make a fresh start at rebuilding American-European institutional relations, particularly in the area of economic affairs. The task becomes even more difficult when one considers the dilapidated foreign service establishment and the despair of the officers who had eagerly welcomed Kissinger as the answer to the Department's prayers.

The question is whether President Ford, burdened by domestic problems, will have the time or the inclination to apply to foreign affairs his contrasting style of openness, reconciliation, and instinct for political compromise. If not, then the force and momentum of Kissinger diplomacy and the popular mystique of the Secretary of State may have a lasting imprint on American foreign policy.

In the coming years America will confront many critical issues in its relations with a uniting Europe. It will have to determine whether its interests will be best served by giving priority to Europe as an entity and as a concept or by sporadic relations with individual European states and by hasty expeditions to cope with immediate crises. If the first option is elected, then there will be the continuing need to insure that problems are managed within the largest political context.

There will be many seductive temptations. Pessimism, confusion, and cross-purpose among the Europeans will foster further skepticism about European unity. Credence will be given to those who urge that America stand aside and leave this subject to Europeans. The inclination to deal with Europe through Bonn, Paris, and London will persist, an American preference reinforced by the instinctive reactions of European leaders. This curious blindness, the superficial ease of dealing with the parts rather than with Europe as a whole, remains despite the accumulated evidence that the smaller countries cannot be ignored, for they have the spoiling capacity to block European and Atlantic actions. The OECD may emerge as the lowest common denominator for Atlantic economic cooperation, the easy course which raises for the nation-states no embarrassing questions of sovereignty. Each of these temptations works against a policy of support for close cooperation with a united Europe.

America must revive its credibility. The threadbare litanies must go. The Europeans must be convinced by indisputable actions that Washington's support for unity is clear and genuine. The policy of support must be exercised with discretion and patience.

A sense of history, a realization of the infinitely complicated process of unification, will be strengthened if Americans can be brought to understand that, in terms of power and political organization, there will exist for the foreseeable future an asymmetrical Atlantic relationship. Neither Europe nor America will find this agreeable. But the imbalance cannot be ignored, nor can the United States escape the burden its greater power imposes. It means that America must continue to exercise leadership and be willing to make marginal sacrifices in recognition of a relationship of unequals.

Another lesson should be drawn from the last decade, the inevitability of the unexpected. We should appreciate the importance of encouraging arrangements between America and Europe to provide some cushion against the sudden crisis and thus to avoid convulsive nationalistic reactions to the unanticipated problems. Formal commitments, informal understandings, processes of consultation, organic arrangements must be part of the web of Atlantic relations designed to manage the unforeseen. If American and European staff contacts are close and sympathetic, an "early warning" system could emerge, making it possible to identify incipient problems to bring them to the political level before they explode on the public scene.

The writing of these pages, in freedom from official restraint but complicated by our chaotic times, in the end has forced me to consider this question: Has the process of intensive analysis altered the conclusions and ideas acquired in years of direct involvement in these affairs? First,

I am resigned to accepting a larger measure of change and disorder than I had felt the system could manage. Second, the message I hoped to convey at the end of 1972, as an uninhibited ex-civil servant—in short, pay attention to Europe, give the forces of unity steady support, and stop being stupid—now seems too simplistic. Yet, third, events have not caused me to alter my assessment of the basic European currents or the compelling reasons for American support for European union. Rather, they have strengthened my sense of the persistently stubborn problems and difficulties in adhering to such a policy. Fourth, I remain impressed by the fact that, behind the turmoil, urgent demands, and conflicts which have cursed Atlantic affairs, lies a deep American and European acknowledgment of mutual dependence. The challenge to political leaders is to transform inarticulated, almost amorphous attitudes into a solid base for more enlightened Atlantic policy.

Finally, I am convinced of the need to develop a new cadre of "believers." This is no tired cry for fresh troops to fight old battles, but for the next generation to examine anew the imperatives of the Atlantic relationship and develop policies to which they will adhere and for which they will fight with the same vigor that marked the efforts of the postwar generation. One fears that we are absent-mindedly producing a breed of elegant, competent, industrious lackeys in the service of pragmatists who see nothing but a world of immediate problems to be solved. The result of this intricate and frenetic bureaucratic patchwork is no policy, no structure, no public understanding, and no public support.

The reconstruction of American policy toward Europe, a policy of imaginative, supple support for unification, will be hard indeed, much harder than the original decision in the early 1950s. Not only must we anticipate a further decline of American interest in international affairs, but also a sense of betrayal as the vaunted achievements of the Nixon-Kissinger era turn out to be less durable and less monumental than bemused spectators were led to believe. Massive economic problems and apparently insoluble political issues set within an Atlantic world of nations at odds with one another permit irritation to grow and gain dominance. We pay dearly for the loss of the wartime and postwar camaraderie which formerly eased tensions and aided the search for common solutions.

In pursuing this project I have discovered a motif of dichotomy; the same people who see clearly the catalog of problems that mark this subject and insist on its careful detail still ask for a more optimistic conclusion. I suspect that this ambivalence cannot be avoided. It would be reckless to ignore the problems related to the European construction, American attitudes and policy, or the dangerous world stage on which these affairs play themselves out. But elements of great strength exist. A more united Europe is undeniably the only means by which the old continent can satisfy its material wants and psychic desires. And in an international environment of gross inequality, of hostility and danger, with America no longer the pre-eminent force of earlier years, we now need a strong and therefore united Europe as never before. I do not question that Americans, if offered leadership, would support policies to this end.

Index